Sharman Macdonald
Plays One

Born in Glasgow, Sharman Macdonald became an actress
on graduation from Edinburgh University but gave it up in
order to write. *When I Was a Girl . . .* won her the
Evening Standard Award for Most Promising Playwright
of 1984 and ran in London for one year. Her novels, *The
Beast* and *Night, Night*, have been published by Collins.
She has written a film script, *Wild Flowers*, which was
made for Channel Four.

SHARMAN MACDONALD

Plays One

*When I Was a Girl, I Used
to Scream and Shout . . .*

When We Were Women

The Winter Guest

Borders of Paradise

Introduced by
the author

faber and faber
LONDON · BOSTON

When I Was a Girl, I Used to Scream and Shout . . . first published in 1985
When We Were Women first published in 1990
This collection first published in 1995 by Faber and Faber Limited
3 Queen Square London WC1N 3AU

Photoset by Parker Typesetting Service, Leicester
Printed in England by Clays Ltd, St Ives plc

A CIP record for this book
is available from the British Library

ISBN 0–571–17621–6

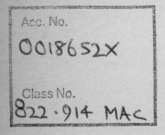
2 4 6 8 10 9 7 5 3 1

Contents

For Robin Don, with love.

Introduction

When I Was a Girl . . . lay on the Edinburgh Traverse Theatre floor for nine months before I made a single phone call to track it down. There must have been piles of plays mounding up there. At that time they didn't have an efficient reader system. I had an argument with Will, my husband, one day. He accused me of not being serious about my writing, of being afraid – how could I let a play go? He was right about the fear; it was and is my biggest handicap. I sent the play to the Bush. I was still acting then. Jenny Topper and Simon Stokes knew me. I didn't want anything to get in the way of the play so I changed my name to Pearl Stewart: Pearl for Janis Joplin and for a great friend who died when she climbed a pyramid – she loved Joplin; Stewart is my middle name. The Bush had and still have an excellent literary department. When the Bush phoned Pearl Stewart about *When I Was a Girl* . . . Will answered the phone. 'Pearl who?' he said. It was as Sharman Macdonald that I had been phoning the Traverse and they never read the play. I had a bet with Will. If I sold the script we'd have another child. She's ten now; still calls herself the Bush baby.

Folk thought I was the daughter in *When I Was a Girl* . . . There are always autobiographical elements in any piece. Plays come out of life after all. But I wasn't Fiona . . . amn't Frances. I wrote *When We Were Women* to knit into the youth of Fiona's mother's generation and because on the opening night of *When I Was a Girl* . . . in the West End Ian Charleson asked me to write a part for him. Writing parts for people doesn't necessarily mean they'll want to play them. Ewan Stewart played

MacKenzie and that was lovely. I remember doing rewrite after rewrite in the corner of the rehearsal room. It was a very happy rehearsal period. None of the rewrites were used and the play remained as it was when I handed it in. I always thought of it as a love play. It's a seductive piece, a dangerous one for a writer to stay close to; so's *The Winter Guest*. I watched *When We Were Women* far too much. I loved the audience's response. I can't watch and create something new. The theatre's Art. I need life to write.

I've never worked on my own. Sure I spend hours sitting alone with a notebook but there's always been people beyond the notebook. Some have been the inspiration for the plays. Some have been given wild words in wild shape to work on while I screamed at them for help. Will made me rewrite the first scene of *When I Was a Girl, I Used to Scream and Shout . . .* fourteen times. I counted. Alan Rickman was sent endless drafts of *The Winter Guest* and wrote long letters about each one. My first drafts are wild. And the second. And the third. Worries me that. I don't see it. I only know it objectively. Someone once told me I had a facility for dialogue and it could be my downfall. I need a work partner and I need to trust him. It has always been a him. I want a dialogue with an audience and sometimes my flurry of verbiage is a barrier to that. Without Will, without Alan, *When I Was a Girl . . .* and *The Winter Guest* wouldn't exist in the form that they do. They would probably never have been done.

Alan Rickman commissioned me to write *The Winter Guest*. It all began with Alan and Lyndsay Duncan at supper. She was talking about her mother, Helen Sinclair Robertson Smith. The stories she told of her mother's illness fascinated Alan. He suggested Lyndsay and I meet. Strange what makes a play happen. In this case it was the fur coat. A daughter shrugging her mother into a fur coat and rubbing the collar up against her face to give her pleasure. The play moved a long way away from Helen and Lyndsay but that moment was always there. But for Alan and, of course, for Helen it wouldn't exist. It's been a joy.

Borders of Paradise feels like the beginning of a new cycle. I left Scotland long ago. *Borders . . .* is the first dialogue piece I've written in English. Scared me to death. The girls are Scottish, the boys are not. Lou Stein had great courage to keep going with me on it. There was one awful day when I phoned him in despair mid-draft and asked why the fuck he'd scheduled it. He just kept telling me how excited he was by the whole idea. The title was his. My title was 'Soft Fall the Sounds of Eden'. Every time I said it people said 'pardon?'. I don't think I've finished with the play yet – I want more music in it, I want to do more work on the first act. It's been thrilling to watch the audiences. They were young. My daughter walked into *Borders . . .* one night. 'Is this a party?' she said. There was a kind of joy in the auditorium. I loved it.

I don't make things up. What I put on the stage never happened in fact but all comes from somewhere in life. I just edit it. My mother ought to be paid royalties. Not that I've ever put her on the stage; just some of the things she's said. She says some rare things. And I've borrowed her extraordinary vitality.

I love watching actors work. I love the whole process, the energy, the commitment, the invention, the courage, the daring. Sian Thomas cut off her lovely hair to play Frances in *The Winter Guest*; Pauline Turner conquered vertigo to perch on a cliff in *Borders of Paradise*; Sandra Voe made Chloe sexy. How did she do that? Kathy Kiera Clarke – I hadn't imagined Ellen the way she played her, now I can't imagine her otherwise. *The Winter Guest* boys left their own world, left home to play Sam and Tom. I was drawn back to the Almeida again and again to watch Phyllida Law play Elspeth. The variation she got into it;

the differences each night; the continual searching; the wonders of the playing of the scene in Act One. Sheila Reid – whenever I think of not writing any more I think of Sheila, of her vitality, and I want to write something else for her. It's all a learning process. With luck the work gets better. After Tat Whalley's audition for *Borders* . . . I rewrote Rob. I wrote him up as I wanted more of Tat on stage. A very fine actor read Ewan for *Borders* . . . but couldn't make him work. I cut Ewan.

I can't talk about my plays without mentioning Robin Don. He designed *When I Was a Girl* . . . and *The Winter Guest*. There was a time when I didn't think *The Winter Guest* would go on. I knew the piece was different. It has no plot after all. Robin phoned up one Sunday morning having just read it. 'I know that beach,' he said. He was determined that the play would go on. I always solve a play's staging problems. I have to know that they can be solved, however crudely. Robin puts magic and beauty on the stage. We saw a model for *The Winter Guest* in his flat, veiled until we had gathered and then revealed, an anglepoise lighting the sky. Perfection. We saw the set being built up in Leeds. And lit. There was a seat on the balcony where shafts of Peter Mumford's light came off the ice in separate beams – in that seat you could practically bathe in the light. Robin's sets are jewels.

I wish the last five months could go on for ever. I've had the best time of my life. I love the people I've worked with and the places I've been. In *Borders of Paradise* Rob says 'Live passionately. Let go lightly.' Complete idiot. Last thing in the world I want to do is to let go of these last five months. I usually dread winter. This year I haven't noticed winter at all.

Sharman Macdonald
May 1995

WHEN I WAS A GIRL, I USED TO SCREAM AND SHOUT . . .

Characters

Morag The mother
Fiona The daughter
Vari The friend
Ewan The boyfriend

The play takes place on a rocky beach on the east coast of Scotland. The set is on two levels. Above is part of a prom, a street light and a railing. Below, a tunnel leads through the façade of the prom to the rocks. Cut into the rocks is a small swimming pool about 4 feet square and waist-height.

When I Was a Girl, I Used to Scream and Shout . . . was first performed at the Bush Theatre, London, in November 1984. The cast was as follows:

Morag Sheila Reid
Fiona Eleanor David
Vari Celia Imrie
Ewan John Gordon Sinclair

Directed by Simon Stokes
Designed by Robin Don
Music by Richard Brown
Lighting by Paul Denby

Act One

SCENE I

1983
The beach.
Fiona *is lying on a towel in a bikini, sunbathing.* **Morag** *is sitting on a travelling rug, surrounded by bags.*

Morag I'm not dressed up. I bought this years ago. Marks and Spencer's. It's a cheap summer dress. It's a nice dress, but it's only cheap. You feel the material. Come on over here and have a feel of this.

Fiona gets up.

Away and don't bother your head. I wouldn't dress up to come down on a beach. I know beaches. All right, these are new. I bought a new pair of sandals to come away for the weekend. What's wrong with that? It's my own wee treat. I'm generous enough with you. I like to look nice. What's wrong with that? I've been well groomed all my life. I'll not stop now. Not even for you. I'll be smart if I want, but as for dressed up . . . What's wrong with you?

Fiona I said, 'You're all dressed up.' I was smiling.

Morag I brought you on this weekend.

Fiona I'm very grateful.

Morag I wanted to see my roses.

Fiona They're not your roses.

Morag I planted them. I tended them. I loved them. But for me there'd be no roses. That house can change hands umpteen times. Those roses are my roses.

5

Fiona All right, they're . . .

Morag A wee holiday.

Fiona Mum . . .

Morag You can say, 'You're all dressed up', or you can say, 'You're all dressed up'.

Fiona You look very smart.

Morag We could have a nice time together. A nice quiet time.

Fiona The colour suits you.

Morag Horse dung, cow dung. I manured those roses with my own hands. All 200 of them. That display is mine.

Fiona It's beautiful.

Morag I thought a nice weekend back here. I've something for you.

Fiona You shouldn't go on spending money.

Morag I mean, if you'd said, 'You're all dressed up'.

Fiona It's a nice dress.

Morag No man, no child, no money. I don't like to see you like this.

Fiona I'm not that bad.

Morag I want to bring the brightness back to your eyes. Here. Come here. Come and see.

> *She brings out a coral necklace. Fiona gets up and goes to the travelling rug.*

Fiona These rocks are burning.

Morag Come on to the travelling rug.

Fiona I'm fine.

Morag You'll burn your bum.

Fiona I'm all right.

Morag Oh, well then. Here. This was yours when you were wee. I had a new clasp put on it. It's coral. Here.

She fastens it round Fiona's neck and hands her a mirror.

What do you think? Of course, it's right in the fashion. You get some colour in your skin.

Fiona It's lovely.

Morag You need a man to give you gold. A gold chain lying with that. You've fine skin. Takes me back. That lying round your neck. Do you want a cup of coffee? I've plenty coffee.

Fiona No.

Morag All those years ago and that lying round your chubby wee neck. Fatty, fatty, fatty but awful bonny. I'm going to have some. (*Pours.*) See that necklace? I was keeping that for my first grandchild.

Fiona You've got a grandchild.

Morag That doesn't count.

Fiona Don't be daft.

Morag I never held him. I never saw him. I mean a proper child. Of my body. Of your body. You're thirty-two, Fiona. A wee head to hold in my hand. A wee head, Fiona. A wee head to hold in my hand.

Fiona Did you bring me here for this?

Morag You're not showing your age.

Fiona Did you?

7

Morag You'll burn your bum on those rocks.

Fiona Am I to have a whole weekend of this?

Morag Your Auntie Nellie had the menopause at thirty. Are you going to tell me you're happy? You've not even got a man. Come on to the rug.

Fiona No.

Morag Every woman needs to have a child. I remember the day I could wear necklaces. You've my neck. I had a good neck. When I was thirty-two, you were five. A woman's body is a clock that runs down very rapidly. You don't need me to tell you that.

Fiona You survived without a man.

Morag Did I? I'm here, that's all you can say. I've loved you all your life. Fiona. No matter what you've done. A wee child to hold in my arms. From your body. From my body. A wee child at my knee.

A voice from inside the swimming pool –

Vari Hey.

Fiona Christ.

Morag I told her you'd be here.

Fiona Thanks.

Morag Away on over with you.

Fiona goes over to the pool

1955
The bedroom.

Vari Willie games?

Fiona She'll see.

Vari Not down here.

Fiona Pencils?

Vari Pencils. (*She holds up two.*)

Fiona Pram covers?

Vari Two fluffy ones with bunny rabbits.

Fiona Excellent.

Vari Willie games?

Fiona Yes.

Vari You come in.

Fiona (*jumps in*) You first.

Vari I was walking along the road, doctor, and I suddenly realized it wasn't there. I've only got a hole. My penis must have dropped off. Can you help me?

Fiona It'll be very sore.

Vari I need my penis back, doctor.

Fiona There's been a great demand this morning. You can have a red penis or a blue penis.

Vari Blue, please.

Fiona Lie down.

Vari Can you find the hole?

Fiona It's huge. This'll hurt. You say, 'Ouch.'

Vari Ouch.

Fiona That's the operation over.

Vari You've kind hands, doctor.

Fiona Thank you.

Vari I'll need a bandage.

Fiona I've a nice fluffy one here.

Vari I like rabbits.

Fiona There.

Vari Oh, doctor, will my new penis take?

Fiona We'll know that tomorrow.

Vari Now you.

Fiona Oh, doctor, I kept wetting the bed and my Mummy said if I didn't stop she'd cut it off. Well, I didn't stop so she did cut it off and it hurt a lot, a lot, a lot. Now I don't wet the bed any more can I have a new penis, please?

Vari You're very lucky I've got one left.

Fiona What colour is it?

Vari Red.

Fiona That'll do nicely, thank you.

Vari Lie down.

Fiona I'm not playing.

Vari I did, you have to.

Fiona I don't want a pencil stuck up me.

Vari It's a penis and I've got one stuck up me. And if it takes I'll be a boy and you won't.

Fiona gets out of the pool. Vari follows.

1983
The beach.

Fiona You were a bloody Queen's Guide. Badges crawling up your arms. The Duke of Edinburgh skulking at your elbow. You made me sick. Always making lemon curd and doing the dusting. You told me there was no Santa Claus. I was sucking a gobstopper. I had just started it. I swallowed it whole. It yo-yoed up and down inside me for days. Cause as soon as you said it I knew it was true. There's no Santa Claus.

Vari So what?

Fiona Waste of a good gobstopper.

Morag What's that bumfle under your skirt, Vari?

Vari Just keeping warm, Auntie Morag.

Morag Never let yourself go, Vari. No matter how tired you are. No matter how depressed you are, you can always have your hair nice and your clothes well brushed. And a bit of lipstick won't break the bank. If your lips look like they'll take a kiss things won't go far wrong. You've put on weight.

Vari I'm always hungry.

Morag How many is it now?

Vari Three.

Morag What age?

Vari Four, three and eight months.

Morag I've something for them. I've three silver bracelets here. They used to be Fiona's. Silver's awful pretty on a baby's skin. You take these. Fiona always had a silver bracelet. I was keeping these for my first grandchild but we're out of luck. Fiona's Auntie Nellie, well, her Great Auntie, my Auntie that was, Auntie Nellie had the menopause at thirty.

Fiona I had a baby.

Morag At least we know you're fertile.

Vari They're lovely. The girls'll be delighted. Thank you very much.

Morag You've not been a mother. You're a sad woman. Look at your eyes.

Vari Look at mine, Auntie Morag, I don't get a night's sleep.

Morag I've a nice cup of tea here. 'The old Bohea,' Fiona's Great Aunt Jean used to say. Her that was Auntie Nellie's sister.

Fiona The bracelets dug into my arm.

Morag When you come down to the beach you've got to be prepared. I bring coffee, tea, sandwiches and cake. And of course the odd bit of fruit and a biscuit or two. I know beaches. (*She begins to lay out a picnic.*)

Vari What have you come here for?

Morag All the sandwiches are on brown bread. I insist on that. I'm not a faddy eater but brown bread is a must in my eyes. Of course Fiona's a vegetarian. So difficult at the hotel.

Fiona We came because she wanted to.

Morag And she doesn't like eggs.

Vari What for?

Morag There's so much nonsense talked about food. Health this and whole that. Fiona's Great Auntie Nellie lived till she was ninety and her favourite food was rare steak covered in cream. Will you have a corned-beef sandwich?

Vari Thank you.

Morag Of course she lost all her hair with the menopause. I've cheese and tomato for you. Apart from that she was healthy.

Fiona No, thank you.

Morag You take it. I'll not see you scraggy. I can count your ribs. A man likes a bit of flesh to puddle his fingers in. Vari's three children are the living proof of that. Hours you'd spend in that bedroom. I could always trust you two to play together. Not like boys. Always with their hands on their dirty wee things. Do you take sugar?

Vari Two, please.

Morag Another sandwich?

Vari Yes, please.

Morag Have you thought of joining the Weight Watchers?

Vari I'm always like this when I'm feeding.

Morag Three children. You'll never be lonely. Be a good daughter to your mother and your children'll do good by you. Eat your sandwich, Fiona, you look drawn.

Fiona You don't look well, Fiona. We're none of us getting any younger, Fiona. You've bags under your eyes, you've wrinkles in your forehead, your wee bit breasts are sagging. Child, menopause, child. It's a mother's place to worry. What else am I going to do? I've all my eggs in the one basket. I didn't want to come back here. What do you want to come back here for?

Morag It was a good place to live.

Fiona If you've something to say to me will you not just say it?

Morag I've lived without a man these past seventeen years. I'm lonely. I want a grandchild.

13

Silence.

Vari These are lovely sandwiches.

Morag I'd say that was my right.

Fiona It is not.

Morag What did I give birth to you for?

Vari Could I maybe have another cup of tea?

Morag Come on to the rug, you'll burn your bum.

Fiona goes to the pool and gets in. Vari follows.

1959
The bathroom.

Vari Do you know where babies come from?

Fiona Up your Auntie Mary. Down the plug-hole.

Vari Do you know how they get in there?

Fiona A woman has a period and a man has a period, sort of, and if they coincide and they happen to be touching, if they're married and they're in bed together then the woman gets a baby.

Vari How do you know that?

Fiona I just do.

Vari See when you get your doings you have to be very careful. I mean if a man touches you then, even if a finger of a man touches you, you might get pregnant.

Fiona My Daddy?

Vari You'll have to keep him off.

Fiona Girls don't get pregnant to their fathers.

Vari Girls are careful. After you've got your doings every

14

time you have a big job, you know the hard kind you have to press out, you mind and look behind you. There might be a baby swimming about there down the bog in amongst the jobbies. So don't pull the flush too quick.

Fiona What else am I going to do with it?

Vari You'd have to love it and take care of it.

Fiona I'm not putting my hand down there to fish it out.

Vari Your Mum likes babies.

Fiona She'd be cross. She's very bad-tempered, my Mum. She'd think I'd been careless.

Vari You'd just have to break it to her gently.

Fiona I think I'd rather pull the flush.

Vari You're disgusting.

Fiona Well, what would you do?

Vari My Mum says always to remember that whatever I do, she'd always love me so never be afraid to tell her anything cause she'd take care of me.

Fiona My Mum said that too.

Vari They're talking about babies.

Fiona I still think they'd be cross.

Vari You've got hairs.

Fiona Where?

Vari Down there. Look.

Fiona Oh, yes. They're nice.

Vari I haven't got any.

Fiona There's six. Daddy, Daddy.

Vari puts her hand over Fiona's mouth.

Vari Let me get out first.

Fiona Daddy, Daddy, Daddy, Daddy, Daddy, Daddy.

Morag jumps up and runs over.

Morag What is it? What is it?

Fiona I've got hair. I've got six hairs. Go and get Daddy.

Morag I thought you'd gone down the plug-hole. The fuss.

Fiona Get Daddy. Get Daddy.

Morag What do you want him for?

Fiona I want him to see. Have I got breasts? Look, I've got bumps. Go and get Daddy.

Morag You can't have your father in the bathroom.

Fiona Why not?

Morag You're very nearly a young lady.

Fiona He'd like to see my hairs.

Morag You must always have your clothes on when you see your Father.

Fiona But my hairs.

Morag I'll tell him.

Fiona You haven't looked.

Morag Very nice.

Fiona They're black. Did you see? Did you? Soon it'll be a forest. That'll be nice. Dorothy hasn't got hair and she's older than me. She says she used to have breasts but they've gone down to get more skin so that they can come back up again.

Morag You're to stop asking your Father to tickle your tummy on a Saturday morning.

Fiona He likes it.

Morag You'll have your doings soon. You'll be a young lady. That'll make Gran proud. Daddies don't tickle the tummies of young ladies.

Fiona You've not to tell Gran. Who'll tickle my tummy? I need my tummy tickled. Don't tell Gran. Promise. I don't want to be a young lady.

Morag It can be the curse indeed.

Fiona I've just got hairs. Don't tell. Don't tell anyone. No one's to know. It'll be a secret, you and me. If I get breasts I'll cross my arms and no one'll know.

Morag We're not great ones for breasts in our family.

Fiona If I don't have them no man'll ever want me.

Morag I did all right. You're a very pretty girl and don't let anyone tell you other. Now. Out of the bath and straight to bed.

Fiona stands up. Morag wraps her in a towel and bustles her to the sunbathing area. Fiona lies down.

1960
The bedroom.

Morag One story, that's all.

Fiona Two.

Morag One, then sleep.

Fiona Two.

Morag We'll see.

Fiona Please. Please.

Morag One.

Fiona Two.

Morag Move over.

Fiona wriggles her bum to take up all the towel.

Move or I'll go downstairs.

Fiona doesn't move. Morag sets off for the tunnel.

Fiona I've moved. Don't go. I've moved. I've moved.

Morag comes back and begins to settle herself beside her daughter on the towel. Fiona is wriggling.

Morag What are you doing?

Fiona Jigging.

Morag Keep still.

Fiona Why?

Morag How jigging?

Fiona Like this.

Morag What's it for?

Fiona Makes me sleepy.

Morag Why?

Fiona Feels nice.

Morag I see.

Fiona Tell me a story.

Morag How nice?

Fiona You know.

Morag I'm hoping I don't know. I'm hoping that you're my own good girl. Are you?

Fiona Yes.

Morag I'm glad. Where does it feel nice?

Fiona Inside.

Morag Where inside?

Fiona Between my legs and up a bit.

Morag It's a bad thing you're doing.

Fiona It makes me sleepy.

Morag I couldn't tell Daddy you were doing this.

Fiona Why?

Morag Now you know there's a God upstairs and he looks down and he sees everything you do.

Fiona I'll only do it in the dark.

Morag God can see in the dark. He sees everything and everyone and if he spots wee Fiona jigging in her bed in the dark, do you know what he does? Do you?

Fiona What does he do?

Morag He looks down and he says to himself, 'That wee Fiona's a naughty, naughty girl and I thought she was one of my better efforts. That wee Fiona's jigging. Tttt. Tttt. Tttt,' he goes. And he calls the Recording Angel. And he says to the Recording Angel, 'I put wee Fiona on the earth to make her mummy happy and look at her now. Jigging. Recording Angel,' says God and the Recording Angel says, 'Yes, Lord.' 'Recording Angel,' says God, 'take up your pen' and the Recording Angel, who's always crying for he has a very sad job, takes up his great big feather pen with the sharp point. 'Recording Angel,' says God, 'open up the book and dip the pen.' The Recording Angel opens the big red book that hangs from his waist by a chain and dips his pen in God's great big inkwell. 'Find wee Fiona's name,' says God and he looks down in his infinite kindness to give you one more chance but you're still jigging away down there in the dark and God blushes for the shame of it and the Recording Angel's tears fall all the faster. And God says, 'Put a black mark at wee Fiona's name, she's a disappointment to me' and the Recording Angel puts a big black mark at your name. And do you know what happens if you get enough black marks? Do you, Fiona?

Fiona No.

Morag You don't go to heaven to pick the flowers in God's green meadows when you die. God casts you down. He looks in his big book and he sees all the black marks. He says, 'I don't want wee Fiona here to dirty up my nice heaven' and he sends you down, all the way down to the devil who's like a snake only worse and the devil sticks you on a spit and roasts you in the fires of hell so he can eat you for dinner.

Fiona Does it hurt?

Morag Oh, yes, it hurts a lot.

Fiona For jigging?

Morag That's right.

Fiona If I stop now do you think God'll say it's all right?

Morag I'm sure he'll be very proud of you.

Fiona I won't do it any more.

Morag That's my good girl. Mummy loves you very much. Mummy will always love you whatever you do.

Fiona What about God?

Morag I'll have a word. Good night. Sleep tight. Don't let the bugs bite.

Morag goes. Vari comes over surreptitiously from the swimming pool and crouches by Fiona's head.

1961
The bedroom.

Vari She's got it all wrong.

Fiona What?

Vari There's no God.

Fiona Yes, there is.

Vari No, there isn't.

Fiona Yes, there is.

Vari I was right about Santa Claus.

Fiona Does that mean it's all right to do it?

Vari No.

Fiona Why?

Vari If you do that your husband'll know when you get married and he'll despise you.

Fiona How will he know? You can't see.

Vari If you keep doing it you go all hard inside. You go like concrete and he can't get in to get his pleasure. So he knows.

Fiona Why does he want to get in?

Vari His penis needs to. It sort of gets up and leads him to the hole and it tries to get in and if it can't the man knows it's your fault and you get divorced. He knows you've been dirty and no man'll live with a dirty lady. He shouldn't be expected to, my Mum says.

Fiona Are you sure his penis goes in?

Vari I've seen.

Fiona Oh, well.

Vari Do you want me to tell you?

Fiona I think I've had enough for one night.

Vari What're you lying all scrunched up for?

Fiona I've got snakes in the bed. They're all round me and I've only got this tiny space to lie in.

Vari That's not very nice.

Fiona They're under the bed too and there's bugs on the wall. But there's a gun where the door handle used to be and if I can reach that I'll be all right.

Vari Did you know your Mum and Dad were getting divorced?

Fiona Is there still a Jesus?

Vari Seems to be proof of that.

Fiona That's nice.

Vari Did you hear me?

Fiona My Mum and Dad are getting divorced.

Pause.

Has she gone all hard inside?

Vari He's got another woman. Who can blame him, my Mum says. Do you believe me?

Fiona Yes. What about me?

Vari My Mum says you've been a bit of a disappointment. My Mum says your Father didn't want a child and your Mum tricked him to get you. Said it was safe when it wasn't.

Fiona My Mum must love me then.

Vari Suppose she must. She won't like her man going though, my Mum says, it's a terrible stigma.

Fiona Are you sure about Jesus?

Vari Oh, yes.

Fiona Does he live in the sky?

Vari He's dead.

Fiona There's not a lot of point in that then.

Vari What?

Fiona I thought he might help with my Mum and Dad.

Vari No chance.

Fiona I'm going to sleep now.

Vari In the dark. I'm scared of the dark.

Fiona So am I.

Vari There's bogies in the dark.

Fiona I know.

Vari They'll get you.

Fiona I know.

Vari We could both get in together, then we'd be all right.

Fiona What do you mean?

Vari I could get in with you. You're awful thick sometimes.

Fiona Why?

Vari Bogies don't attack you when you're with someone.

Fiona Why not?

Vari Never mind why not. They don't, that's all. But if you want the bogies to get you, that's your tough tof.

Fiona OK then.

Vari OK then what?

Fiona Get in.

Vari I don't know if I want to now.

Fiona Och, Vari, come on.

Vari Bogies cling to the wall and drop on your face and they suffocate you. It's a horrible death, my Mum says.

Fiona Gonnie get in?

Vari Say 'Please'.

Fiona Please.

Vari Move, then. (*Vari gets into the towel bed.*) Are you sure there's snakes in here?

Fiona Yes.

Vari I can't feel them.

Fiona They're only here for me.

Vari Right, I'm comfy.

Fiona Good.

Vari I've an idea.

Fiona What?

Vari Do you want to know what it's like when a man and woman do it?

Fiona Eh?

Vari Do you?

Fiona What, now?

Vari Why not?

Fiona How?

Vari I'll be the man and you be the woman.

Fiona What do I do?

Vari Take your jammies off.

Fiona I will not.

Vari Shhhhh. Shhhhh. Do you want everyone to hear? It's only sensible to practise. We've got to make it as real as possible. I mean, you don't think they do it with their clothes on, do you?

Fiona I don't know.

Vari Well, they don't. It's only sensible. How can his thing go in you if you've got a pair of pyjamas in the way? That's what's known as contraception.

Fiona Sorry.

Vari I've got mine off. Hurry up.

Fiona Ready.

Vari Right. I'm going to kiss your ear.

Fiona Why?

Vari That's what they do. Ready?

Fiona Yes.

Vari kisses Fiona's ear.

Vari Right. That's that bit. Was it nice?

Fiona Yes.

Vari Now I'm going to kiss your mouth.

Fiona No.

Vari I've got to.

Fiona I don't want you to.

Vari It won't work if we don't do it properly.

Fiona I don't like it.

Vari All right, we'll skip the mouth bit. I'll just get on top of you.

Fiona No.

Vari Do you want to practise or not?

Fiona All right.

Vari Right. Try to just concentrate, will you. I mean you'd think we were doing something dirty.

Fiona Sorry.

Vari Right. (*Gets on top of Fiona.*) How's that? Am I heavy?

Fiona No. Not really.

Vari Do I feel nice?

Fiona I suppose so.

Vari Don't be so enthusiastic. I mean, I'm the one doing all the work.

Fiona Sorry.

Vari Right. I haven't got one so I'll just jig up and down a bit.

Fiona Jigging.

Vari What?

Fiona Stop.

Vari I don't want to.

Fiona It's jigging, Vari. God'll see.

Vari There's no God.

Fiona It feels like jigging.

Vari I told you there's no God.

Fiona Aye. But what if there is?

Vari What if?

Fiona He'll look down and he'll see. Get off.

Vari Not now.

Fiona Get off.

Vari Do you mean it?

Fiona I mean it. I mean it. Get off.

Vari I won't be your best friend any more.

Fiona Sorry.

Vari So am I.

Fiona Will you be able to sleep?

Vari I can always sleep.

Fiona I really am awful sorry.

Vari I'll just find someone else to practise with and you'll feel an awful idiot when you have to do it for real and you don't know how.

Fiona Who will you find?

Vari I'm not telling.

Fiona Go on.

Vari You're just like your Mum. My Mum says you can't hold back on a man. You won't keep a man either.

Fiona My Mum says you've got to keep your kisses for the man you love and if you don't you're cheap and you didn't say there wasn't a devil and the devil gets you for jigging and that's a well-known fact and I don't care what you say we were jigging. I've got enough to contend with with bugs and bogies, never mind asking the devil to pay a visit too. Now you go home. I've a busy night ahead of me. I've 345 snakes in this bed and I've got to kill them all by morning and I haven't even reached the gun yet.

Vari You're a prude, Fiona McBridie.

Fiona Go away.

Vari You just see if I care. (*half goes*) You're going to be half an orphan as good as and nobody'll like you any more.

Blackout.

SCENE 2

1983
The beach. Bright sunlight.
Morag is on the rug. Fiona is drying herself.

Fiona Well?

Morag Is it your business?

Fiona He was my Dad. You're my Mother.

Morag You've never asked before.

Fiona I was very young when he went.

Morag That's about the sum of it.

Fiona What?

Morag When your father left I was thirty-seven. I was very grateful to him that I wasn't forty. And that was my chief emotion. I knew he was going to go. All I prayed was that he'd not hang it out. It's a different thing trying to get another man at forty. At thirty-seven I even had another baby in me. Maybe. If some man hurried up.

Fiona Why didn't you leave him?

Morag I loved him but if he went I didn't want to spend the rest of my life without a man. I like men. Not sex, you understand. That's dirty. Your father was like an elephant, if he got it once in ten years he could consider himself lucky. So he went. I could never see anything in it. With the telly now I can see I must have been wrong. I mean, there wouldn't be such a fuss if there was nothing in it.

Fiona That's sad.

Morag Not in the least. You're thirty-two and you've not got a child. That's sad.

Fiona I don't want one.

Morag Rubbish.

Fiona I don't.

Morag Every woman wants a child.

Fiona Not me.

Morag It's not as if your career's a success.

Fiona It might be.

Morag I'm paying for this holiday.

Fiona I only came to keep you company.

Morag I only came because you were looking so awful I thought you'd never get a man and that's all the thanks I get.

Fiona I've got several men.

Morag Don't be dirty.

Fiona Well, I have.

Morag Where are they then? I don't see them.

Fiona They sure as hell aren't on the east coast of Scotland having a quiet weekend with my Mother, being intruded on by a best friend I haven't seen for seventeen years.

Morag Are you a lesbian?

Pause.

Don't look at me like that. I'm only asking.

Fiona I didn't even know you knew the word.

Morag Don't be silly. My own sister was one, of course I know the word.

Fiona Who?

Morag Jane.

Fiona Jane's married.

Morag Oh, aye, she did eventually but that was after.

Fiona What?

Morag You haven't answered me.

Fiona What?

Morag Are you a lesbian?

Fiona I'm not going to answer you.

Morag I won't tell you about your Aunt Jane.

Fiona Stuff you then.

Morag Don't talk to your Mother like that. It was a civilized question. I expect a civilized answer.

Fiona No, I'm not a lesbian, I just don't want a baby. Now, what about Auntie Jane?

Morag I thought I'd have known about it. I mean you've ruined my life with your other problems. I suppose you'd have found some way to let me know about that. You know what I'm talking about.

Pause.

Fiona Tell me about Auntie Jane.

Morag Of course your Grandmother was appalled, sort of.

Fiona Did she know?

Morag They did it under her roof. I always thought that was most unwise. Your Grandmother threw them out, told them to book into a hotel but she didn't want the sounds of their pleasure coming through her bedroom ceiling. It was bad enough with a man. It was an ATS sergeant. Your Auntie Jane was between twenty and thirty and single in the war years so she got conscripted. She'd have gone anyway. She liked the uniform and she was awful patriotic. That's why she emigrated to South Africa and not because of the scandal as some thought.

Fiona What scandal?

Morag It was whispered up and down our street. The ATS sergeant was crop-haired. She had a low voice and a flat chest. She and Jane walked around arm in arm. The ATS sergeant was never out of uniform and Jane had always had a softness for frills. It was awful obvious. But that was when the bombs were falling on Clydebank and Glasgow. Your Grandmother relented. She thought her children should have their pleasure before a bomb got them. Whatever their pleasure might be. She didn't insist they left the house, just moved them to another bedroom so she didn't have to listen. Then they were next to me so that's how I knew for certain. I thought it might run in the family.

Fiona What have we come here for?

Morag Well, that's a relief. I didn't quite know what kind of a face I was going to put on it if you were.

Fiona Answer me.

Morag What, dear?

Fiona Why have we come here?

Morag For a rest, dear.

1966
The beach.
Vari runs down the rocks.

Vari Five numbers. One, two, three, four, five. One for kissing. Two for tongue in the mouth. Three for breast. Four for fingers. Five for your hand on him.

Fiona What's after five?

Pause.

Vari Six.

Fiona What's number six?

Vari It goes up to ten.

Fiona What are the others?

Vari Don't be dirty.

Fiona You don't know.

Vari How far have you gone?

Fiona How far have you gone?

Vari You first.

Fiona No, you.

Vari I asked you first.

Fiona I asked you second.

Vari Scaredy cat. I won't tell. I know. You're a whore.
You've been to ten and back again. Only whores go to ten.

Fiona Don't be silly.

Vari Apart from mothers.

Fiona What's number four?

Vari His fingers up you.

   Silence.

You're dirty.

Fiona I didn't say I had, I just asked what it was.

   Silence.

What do his fingers do up you?

Vari Don't be daft.

Fiona What do they do?

Vari You know.

Fiona What?

Vari Wiggle about a bit.

Fiona What does it feel like?

Vari Haven't you ever . . .? You know.

Fiona What?

Vari Done it to yourself.

Fiona No. Should I? Is it nice?

Vari It's all right.

Fiona Is it nice when he does it?

Vari Promise you won't tell.

Fiona Promise.

Vari Promise.

Fiona Promise.

Vari I've only done it once.

Fiona When?

Vari I'm telling you. Shut up. It was here. Up by the tunnel. Last Saturday. I was allowed out to eleven so . . .

Fiona Ten o'clock, me.

Vari Do you want to hear? We got down here and we were holding hands and that was a bit boring. I mean, he's not a great conversationalist.

Fiona He's got lovely legs. And a black PVC raincoat.

Vari We sat on that. It was warm last Saturday.

Fiona Could you smell the shit from the sewers? I never think that's very romantic. What's wrong?

Vari I'm just thinking I'm not going to tell you.

Fiona I'm sorry.

Vari You're always sticking your oar in.

Fiona What did he stick?

They giggle and they giggle.

Vari Anyway he kissed me. You know nice little nibbling ones not the great wet open-mouthed kind you get from some of them. Nice little nibbling things on the corner of my mouth and just down a bit. Then he put his tongue in my mouth and that got a bit boring so I took his hand and put it on my breast. My right breast, I think it was. He seemed to like that though he didn't do much. Then that got a bit boring so I put my hand on his thing. Don't look like that. There comes a time when you've got to, you know, take things into your own hands. So I did. I mean I'd never seen one except on statues. Anyway tit for tat. He was groping away so why shouldn't I? It was all hard. I suppose I should have expected that but it was an awful shock. I sort of rubbed away a bit. Then he did it. He got it out. He undid his trousers and out it came.

Pause.

Fiona Well?

Vari It was very big. How does that ever fit into you? It was all sort of stretched and a bit purple. Though I couldn't see very well. It seemed rude to stop and stare. I mean if you've got something like that I don't suppose you really want it looked at. He didn't. Cause he got on top of me. He pushed me over. He pulled up my skirt. He stuck his fingers up inside my pants and inside me. Then he rubbed a bit, you know, himself up and down on me. Then he sort of gasped and stopped. There was this great wet patch on my skirt when I got up. I told my Mum I'd dropped my ice-cream, you know, old-fashioned vanilla. Say something. Go on. You think I'm dirty.

Fiona I don't.

Vari You do.

Fiona I was just wondering what number it was that you got to.

Ewan, *long-legged and in black PVC, comes to the mouth of the tunnel.*

Vari Look.

Fiona It's him.

Vari Go on, he knows what to do. You try him.

Fiona Me?

Vari You like his legs.

Fiona Another time.

Vari Sure.

Fiona He's waving to you.

Vari There was this great lump of rock sticking in my back. I've got a bruise.

Vari goes off through the tunnel with Ewan.

1966
The bathroom.

Morag (*calling from the bath*) Bring me my clothes and get yourself in here. I'll not call again.

Fiona Here.

Morag Sit down, I want a word.

Fiona (*sits gingerly*) What?

Morag I'm forty-two years old.

Fiona Did I not remember your birthday?

Morag Don't be daft. You don't look very comfortable.

Fiona I'm all right. What do you want?

Morag Your Father left five years ago.

Fiona I know that. (*She shifts, stands up, smooths her skirt at the back.*)

Morag Will you keep still, I'm trying to talk to you. Here, hold the towel, I'm getting out. (*She gets out. She's in a bathing suit. She drapes the towel.*) Here, look at me. I'm no half bad. I've always had a good figure, no one can deny me that. I've done my exercises through morning and night. My stomach's like a board. No baggy skin and I never had any breasts so you won't see them sagging. If you cut off my head you'd think I was nineteen. Pity about my head. If I had money I'd go straight to a plastic surgeon. A wee pull here, a stretch there. You've got St Vitus's dance.

Fiona You're a very attractive woman.

Morag Thank you, Fiona. Grooming. Always be smart. Even if you're poor your clothes can be well brushed. You've not been still since you came in here.

Fiona Sorry.

Morag We've always had a good relationship, you and me. Well? We have, haven't we?

Fiona Yes.

Morag So. As I say, your Father left five years ago.

Fiona Yes.

Morag Oh, Fiona, I've found a man. I'm in love. I never really thought it would happen to me. I say I found him. He really found me. I feel seventeen. I'm happy. I'm going to ask him to the house and I wanted very humbly to ask your permission. I want him to come to dinner and I wanted you to meet him. What do you say?

Fiona I've run out of sanitary towels.

Morag Pardon?

Fiona I'm on the last one in the house and that's nearly through. I'm going to get blood on my skirt.

Morag Go and buy some.

Fiona You didn't order them from the Co-op.

Morag I forgot.

Fiona You always order them with the messages.

Morag My mind wasn't on it. Can he come to dinner?

Fiona What am I going to do?

Morag Put your coat on. Get some at the corner shop.

Fiona No.

Morag Don't be daft. You can't not have sanitary towels. That's dirty.

Fiona Have you slept with him?

Morag There's money in my purse.

Fiona I can't.

Morag Don't be stupid.

Fiona There's a man in the corner shop.

Morag Men know women have periods.

Fiona But he'll know it's actually coming out of me now. I'll be standing there bleeding in his shop and he'll know.

Morag Wait for the woman to come out from the back.

Fiona You go.

Morag I will not.

Fiona You're the one who forgot.

Morag You're the one who's bleeding.

Fiona But I'm not a woman.

Morag Get the money from my purse and get along to that shop before you spoil your nice clothes.

Fiona No.

Morag It'll be closed soon and then where'll you be?

Fiona Bloody.

Morag You watch your tongue.

Fiona I'm not going. You're my Mother. You're supposed to take care of me.

Morag You'll feel the back of my hand.

Fiona I won't go. You forgot. You forgot.

Morag (*dressing*) I saw you when you were born. Two hours I was in labour with you and you ripped me right up to my bum. You came out from between my legs and your eyes were open. You knew exactly what you'd done. The midwife held you up. You looked right at me. You didn't cry. No, madam. Not you. You gave me look for look. I didn't like you then and I don't like you now. Do you hear me, Fiona? Are you listening, Fiona? I don't like you. Nasty little black thing you were. You had hair to your

shoulders and two front teeth. You wouldn't suck. I tried
to feed you. I did everything that was proper. You'd take
nothing from me. Your father took you. He dandled you
and petted you. You had eyes for him all right. Well, he's
not here now. You won't find him down at the corner shop
buying your sanitary towels. I took care of you. I clothed
you and washed you and you had your fair share of
cuddles. Sometimes I even quite liked you. Though you've
gone your own way. You smoke, don't you? Don't you
look at me like that. You walk back from that school every
day, save the bus money for cigarettes. I know you do. I've
seen you. I've not said. I've not said all I know about you.
You sat on your father's knee, you clapped his head, you
could get anything you wanted. You thought you could.
You thought you could. You're still just a wee girl.
Hanging round the prom on a Sunday teatime. I've seen
you. Hanging round the boys. I've seen you, butter
wouldn't melt in your mouth with your Sunday morning
piety fresh on you and a smell of smoke on your breath.
I've seen you looking at them. Sleekit smile on your face.
You know it all. Well, do you, my girl? Do you know it
all? You live in my house and in my house you do as I say,
and if anything happens to you with your sly ways you'll
not stay in my house. You'll be out the door and you'll not
come back. What you ask for you get. Now go and buy
your sanitary towels.

Silence.

I'm sorry. I love you. I'll always love you. I'm just out of
the bath, Fiona. Are you asking me to catch my death?

Fiona You've gone to bed with him.

Morag I'll not have you spreading blood on my furniture.

Fiona You've let him touch you.

Morag Get the sanitary towels.

Fiona It's a sin what you've done.

Morag Get to that shop.

Fiona You're a sinner.

Morag Get.

Fiona You're a whore.

Morag hits Fiona hard. Morag goes to the towel. She picks up a coat and goes down the tunnel.

1966
The beach.

Vari (*popping up*) Why did you not just go?

Fiona It's dark.

Vari So what?

Fiona I'm scared of the dark.

Vari If she gets a cold where'll you be?

Fiona I don't care.

Vari She wants to go away.

Fiona Who?

Vari Auntie Morag.

Fiona Why?

Vari Her man's got a job abroad. He's in oil. He's got to go to some Arab country or other. He wants her to go with him and she wants to go.

Fiona She does not.

Vari She does so.

Fiona What about me?

41

Vari You're not liable to get to university via the Trucial States so she asked my Mum if you could live with us, as a paying guest, seeing as we're friends.

Fiona I don't want to live with you.

Vari Why not?

Fiona I want to live in my own house with my own mother. She can't go pissing off. She's responsible for me. She loves me.

Vari She loves her man.

Fiona When did she talk to your Mum?

Vari The day before yesterday.

Fiona Why didn't she tell me first?

Vari She guessed how well you'd take it.

Fiona I'll live with my Dad. He loves me.

Vari Your Dad's got three wee kids of his own.

Fiona I'm his own.

Vari It's not an option.

Fiona My Dad loves me.

Vari Your Mum's checked it out. He doesn't want you. He said you could go for the odd weekend. You're not that easy to get on with. Adolescents never are.

Fiona Where are the Trucial States?

Vari On the Persian Gulf.

Fiona There's oil here.

Vari It's hotter over there and you don't have to live in the middle of the sea.

Fiona She's a whore.

Vari That's what my Mum says. My Mum says that them that come to it late are insatiable.

Fiona It's my Dad's bed.

Vari She doesn't want to live on her own for the rest of her life. My Mum's jealous. I don't think sex with my Dad's a party.

Fiona I'm not going to let her go.

Vari You can't stop her.

Fiona I can.

Vari How?

Fiona I'll stop her.

1983
The beach.

Morag Oh, my God, would you look at that?

Fiona It's a jellyfish.

Vari Oh, God.

Fiona It's not doing you any harm.

Morag I'll be the judge of that.

Vari It's oozing, Auntie Morag.

Morag Get rid of it.

Fiona What for?

Vari It's obscene.

Morag I'm not sitting on the same beach as that.

Fiona Oh, for goodness' sake.

Vari It's all jelly.

Morag You. You wouldn't even kill a wasp. What are you doing?

Fiona has taken the sandwich container.

Fiona Getting rid of it.

Morag You're not using that.

Fiona You do it.

Morag That's a good sandwich box. I've used that year in, year out.

Fiona It'll wash.

Morag Don't be so damned silly. I couldn't eat out of that again. It's sullied.

Vari I stepped on a slug once, in the dark with my bare foot.

Morag When Fiona was a wee girl, she dived on top of a jellyfish in this very water. You'd think she'd show some sensitivity about my sandwich box.

Fiona It's still alive.

Morag Spread its jelly all over her. Arms, legs, chest and face. Bright red she went and burning with fever. What are you doing?

Fiona Putting it in the pool.

Vari Oh, God, Fiona.

Fiona The tide'll take it away.

Morag You might at least do the decent thing and stick it in a litter bin.

Fiona I'm not killing it.

Morag Oh, for goodness' sake. Give it here. Give it to me.

Fiona I will not.

Morag That's my box. Give it to me.

Fiona gives up the box.

I should think so.

Morag marches off to find a litter bin.

Fuss about a damn jellyfish.

Vari Slugs, worms and jellyfish. I hate them.

Blackout.

Act Two

SCENE I

1966
The beach. The sun is shining.
Ewan comes in from the sea. He settles on the hot rock.
Fiona comes on to the rocks through the tunnel. She's in
her bikini. She sees Ewan. She creeps to the pool and
gathers water in her hands. She moves over to Ewan and
drops the water on him.

Ewan (*screams*) Fucking cunt.

Fiona moves away from him and sits staring out to sea.
Ewan dries himself meticulously.

Jesus Christ, woman. What do you expect, creeping up on
a man like that? Took my breath away. I mean, Jesus,
Fiona. That water's freezing. It's not the bloody
Mediterranean. What the hell do you have to play bloody
stupid games for? I mean, shit, Fiona. Come on. What's a
man supposed to do? I mean, shit, Fiona. Shit.

Pause.

Come here. Look at the bloody face on it. Come here. I
forgive you. Come on, I'll give you a cuddle. Bloody hell,
woman. Bloody listen, will you. Move your backside over
here. I've said I forgive you. Jesus Christ, what do you
fucking well want? Dear God, woman, it's not as if I
sodding well hit you. I mean, if I'd hit you you'd have
something to bloody girn about. Don't be bloody
ridiculous.

Pause.

46

You want me to say sorry to you. You sodding well do.
You do. I sodding well won't. You've not a pissing hope.
Shit.

Pause.

I'm fucking sorry. There. Is that bloody better?

Fiona moves over to him.

Bloody smile then.

Fiona My Mum's going with a man.

Ewan She's pretty, your Mum. I could fancy her.

Fiona They sleep together in our house.

Ewan Where do you expect them to go?

Fiona It's disgusting.

Ewan She's not that old, your Mum. Women probably
need it as well as men. Your Dad left a long time ago.

Fiona Shut up.

Ewan It'd do you good.

Fiona I'm not sixteen.

Ewan What about it though?

Fiona What?

Ewan I could come to your house when your Mum's at
work.

Fiona My bedroom's at the front.

Ewan That's nice for you. You'll have a sea view.

Fiona Everyone'll see if I close the curtains during the day.

Ewan Is that what's stopping you?

Fiona They'll see you coming in, someone will even if you go round the back and if I close the curtains they'll know exactly what we're doing. The boy across the road hangs his penis out his upstairs window in his bare scuddy. The woman next door warned my Mum so that I wouldn't look but he only does it for me so it seems awful rude not to. He's always looking out for me so he can do it. He'd tell. The woman next door's got the police to him three times. She says she's got an interest in my welfare and he's a traffic hazard. He'd tell to get his own back. He thinks it's my fault he does it. You know, for being there. He was born in his house and we moved into ours and my bedroom's really the dining room so I shouldn't be there anyway. That's what he thinks. I'm always getting flashed at.

Ewan Want a look?

Fiona Don't be daft.

Ewan You're very pretty.

Fiona Thanks.

Ewan Give us a kiss.

> *Morag is on the prom. Fiona and Ewan are necking on the rocks.*

Morag Fiona. Come here. Come here.

Fiona Oh, Christ.

Ewan Leave this to me. Stay there.

Fiona I'll have to come.

Ewan I'll deal with it.

Fiona All right but I'm coming too.

Morag Move yourself, Fiona.

They join Morag above.

What do you think you're doing, the pair of you? You're in public.

Ewan I must apologize, Mrs McBridie, it was entirely my fault.

Morag You were both getting your lips wet.

Ewan At my behest.

Morag Indeed. And who are you?

Ewan Ewan Campbell. I live up the Crescent.

Morag Do you?

Ewan I do.

Morag You'll be the one at the bus stop in the uniform of the Academy.

Ewan I've often admired your roses.

Morag Och, away with you. I know fine what you're trying to do. You won't get round me.

Ewan Will you accept my apologies for kissing your daughter in public?

Morag You were half-way down her throat. If that was kissing times have changed.

Ewan You've changed with them.

Morag Have I?

Ewan May I take your daughter to the cinema?

Morag I said she wasn't to go out with a boy till she was sixteen.

Fiona Please, Mum.

Morag You'll sit in the chummies and smooch all the way through the film.

Ewan We'll endeavour to give you a good account of the story afterwards.

Morag I'll expect you to the house for tea before you go. Don't let me down again, the pair of you. There's plenty of time for that sort of thing when you're older.

Fiona Your age.

Morag Mind your mouth.

Ewan I'll be seeing you on Saturday then?

Fiona Yes.

Ewan Goodbye, Mrs McBridie.

Morag Aye.

Ewan goes out through the tunnel.

I want to talk to you.

Fiona You were flirting with him.

Morag I'd be trying to get off with him right enough.

Fiona I didn't want him to come to the house.

Morag I'm sorry. I thought he was your friend.

Fiona You can have your man there and we'll be a cosy wee foursome. You can have one on either side and show off your winsome ways. Flutter your eyelashes.

Morag You've a cheap tongue.

Fiona You wanted me.

Morag Yes.

Fiona Is this it?

Morag What?

Fiona You're going away.

Pause.

Why didn't you tell me?

Morag I couldn't.

Fiona You're a whore and you're not even brave.

Morag Don't speak to me like that.

Fiona Why didn't you tell me?

Morag I want to sell the house and go with him.

Fiona I won't let you.

Morag In two years you'll be at university. I don't want to spend the rest of my life on my own.

Fiona I might want to go to university here.

Morag You'll not want to stay with me.

Fiona You're supposed to take care of me.

Morag If I could take you with me I would.

Fiona Would you?

Morag I love you very much.

Fiona You don't love me. Love. You love yourself. You love your reflection in a man's eyes. The first man that comes along you abandon me. Fuck you, Mother.

Morag Fiona.

Fiona I don't want him in the house. (*She runs down to the beach.*)

1966
The beach.

Vari What are you going to do? Have you decided?

Fiona Know any good jokes?

Vari What?

Fiona I could do with a laugh.

Vari What are you going to do?

Fiona Right, I'll tell you one.

Vari Is it dirty?

Fiona Maybe.

Vari Go on.

Fiona I'm going to get pregnant.

Vari You are not.

Fiona I am so.

Vari You can't.

Fiona Wait and see.

Vari Is that the joke?

Fiona It'll stop her.

Vari How will it?

Fiona She can't go and leave me with a baby. I'm fifteen. What would people say? She'd care about that though she doesn't give a shit about me.

Vari You'll wreck your life.

Fiona No, I won't.

Vari Who's going to do it?

Fiona Ewan Campbell. Do you mind?

Vari Does he? Do you fancy him?

Fiona He's all right.

Vari Why don't you come and stay with us?

Fiona Your Mum's a bitch.

Vari She's two-faced. She'd only be nasty behind your back. You can't sleep with someone you just think's all right.

Fiona I thought you'd think it was a good idea.

Vari It's a terrible idea.

Fiona You've gone with him.

Vari I'm a virgin and that's the way I'm going to stay till I get married which I'll do when I'm twenty-six, and have three very quick children and be back to work 'cause I'm not going to be a skivvy like my Mum. My man'll have enough money to buy a woman to do for me and private nurseries.

Fiona What's the point in having them then?

Vari You've got to have babies.

Fiona Right.

Vari Not when you're fifteen.

Fiona Watch me. I'll be here on Saturday night after the film. It's the right time in my menstrual cycle. I'll get pregnant.

Vari You know an awful lot suddenly.

Fiona I've been to the library.

Vari You've not to do it.

Fiona She'll bloody stay. I won't live on my own. She'll bloody stay.

1983
The beach.

Morag (*from above*) I've brought ice-cream cones. You can't have a holiday without ice-cream cones. Where are your three lovely children?

Vari My Mum takes them for a morning sometimes.

Morag That'll give you a wee break. She'll be very proud of you, your Mum.

Vari Sorry?

Morag Your big house and your fine doctor husband.

Vari She thinks I'm mad.

Morag Why is that, dear?

Vari I went in for Shona, my third. I told her. She didn't speak to me for six months. Said if I wanted to ruin my life it was my affair.

Morag I see.

Vari Look at me. I'm fat. I've seen you, Fiona. You can't keep your eyes off my tummy. I strip myself at night. He's not often there so no one sees. I look at myself in the mirror. This is a mother's body. Where am I? Don't think I pity myself. I wanted this from when I was wee. I'm feeling puzzled. Where am I? My tits have got great blue veins running across them. They look good when they're full of milk but then it's mostly running down my front so the effect's somewhat spoilt. When they're empty they're poor things. All the exercises in the world'll not save my stomach. The doctor's face when I'd had Moira. He pulled out a handful of skin. I said that'll go away won't it. He let it go. Splat. He shook his head. He looked awful sad. He probably knows Archie. Felt sorry he had to make love to a doughbag for the rest of his life. I mean, I could have an operation. Archie's said already about it. They take away all the stretched-out skin. You end up looking like a hot cross bun. They cut you from here to here and up. I'd rather buy a corset. I mean, God or no God, you're asking for it if you fiddle. I mean, I'm healthy. You can have it on the National Health, the operation. Archie wouldn't compromise his principles even for the sake of his own pleasure. There's always divorce.

Morag What God's intended God's appointed.

Fiona Don't say that.

Vari Listen, it's easier if he's not there. I can handle the children. I eat what they eat. We get on fine. When he's in he enquires politely about the mess, makes requests about the level of the noise and I have to cook him dinner. It's not his fault. He's got his work. He likes a cooked breakfast too. Archie's very good to me. He lets the babies sleep in the bed with me and he goes to another room. We're lucky we have a good big house. That way he gets his sleep and I only have to turn over when they wake in the night. Of course we don't make love but I wake up covered in milk and piss, I can do without sperm as well. I beg your pardon, Auntie Morag.

Fiona Do you miss sex?

Vari I've read every book in existence on the female orgasm. I've never had one.

Morag Still. We'll get into heaven.

Pause.

You're very quiet, Fiona.

Pause.

Though you're my own daughter and I love you, I have to say it. You were always common.

Morag throws a travelling rug round her shoulders and slowly leaves. Vari and Fiona sit in the gloaming of evening.

1966
The beach.
Ewan comes in through the tunnel.

Ewan Where are you? Stop playing bloody silly games.

Fiona I'm here.

Vari moves into the shadows.

Ewan Where did you get the towel?

Fiona I left it here this afternoon.

Ewan It'll be damp.

Fiona The rocks keep their heat.

Ewan What number do you go to?

Fiona I go up to ten and back again.

Ewan Christ.

Fiona It's your lucky night.

Ewan Are you serious?

Fiona Yes.

Ewan I haven't got a thing.

Fiona What?

Ewan French letter.

Fiona Never mind.

Ewan Are you kidding me?

Fiona No.

Ewan You're not one of them?

Fiona What?

Ewan They're low.

Fiona Who?

Ewan PTs.

Fiona No.

Ewan You're not a virgin then?

Fiona Do you want to do it?

Ewan I think so.

Fiona Make up your mind.

Ewan I'm surprised.

Fiona Have you done it before?

Ewan I've gone quite far.

Fiona Right then.

Ewan What?

Fiona Let's start.

Ewan Are you sure it's safe?

Fiona Do you want to or not?

Ewan Are you going to take your clothes off?

Fiona It's not that warm.

Ewan You don't sound very excited.

Fiona Neither do you.

Ewan It takes a bit of getting used to.

Fiona You do fancy me?

Ewan Yes. Yes, of course I do.

Fiona Do you think I'm cheap for wanting to do it?

Ewan I respect you.

Fiona Right then. We could kiss first.

Ewan Yes, of course.

Vari creeps up as they kiss.

Vari That doesn't look very exciting.

Fiona It's not.

Vari Better do something.

Fiona What?

Vari Bite his ear.

Fiona That's not very original.

Vari Just do it.

Fiona bites Ewan's ear.

His hand moved. Stick your tongue in.

Fiona Where?

Vari His ear, stupid. Go on.

Fiona does as she's told.

Has he got a hard-on?

Fiona I don't know.

Vari Find out.

Fiona How?

Vari Do you want me to do it for you?

Fiona No.

Vari Stick your hand on it.

Fiona does.

Don't be so rough. Is it hard?

Fiona I think so.

Vari Lie down.

Fiona Where?

Vari On your back.

Fiona I haven't any knickers on. Do you think he'll get a fright?

Vari How do I know?

Fiona You practically did it with him.

Vari What did you take your knickers off for?

Fiona I thought they'd get in the way.

Vari He's puffing a bit. His hand's moved right up your leg.

Fiona This is quite exciting.

Vari Lie down quick.

Fiona moves away from Ewan and lies on the towel.

Fiona He hasn't touched my tit yet. He should, shouldn't he?

Vari It's not compulsory.

Fiona I thought you had to.

Vari Considering what you're offering a tit's a bit tame.

Ewan moves on top of Fiona.

Fiona Is this it?

Vari Has he got it out?

Fiona I don't know.

Vari You must know.

Fiona What if he comes before it's in?

Vari I don't know. Do you like it?

Fiona Yes. Ouch.

Vari What?

Fiona It's in.

Vari You're dirty.

Fiona You can go.

Vari goes.

Ewan You were a virgin.

Fiona So were you.

Ewan You must love me an awful lot.

Fiona Do you want to do it again?

Ewan Why?

Fiona Didn't you like it?

Ewan Yes, but . . .

Fiona What?

Ewan Did you?

Fiona Yes. Well. Very nearly.

Ewan You're not supposed to, are you?

Fiona Why not?

Ewan You're female. Whores enjoy it.

Fiona Are you saying I'm a whore?

Ewan I don't know, do I?

Fiona I was a virgin.

Ewan Do you love me?

Fiona No, I don't.

Ewan What did you do it for then?

Fiona You're not to tell anyone.

Ewan I won't.

Fiona If I hear you've told; if I hear a word about this night on the beach, I'll say you couldn't do it.

Ewan I thought it would be different.

   Pause.

Are you angry with me?

Fiona You're the only other one here.

Ewan What did you do it for?

Fiona You did it too.

Ewan Will I see you again?

Fiona I'll be getting the bus on Monday morning.

Ewan I mean see you.

Fiona I know fine what you mean.

Ewan Well?

Fiona Go home, Ewan.

Ewan I promised your Mum I'd see you safe to your front door.

Fiona What could happen to me?

Ewan You know.

Fiona Tell me.

Ewan What's up with you?

Fiona Tell me.

Ewan Rape. Fiona. I could give you a cuddle.

Fiona Och, Ewan, it'll not fix itself. Go away and leave me alone.

Ewan Come here.

Fiona Just go away, will you. Please.

Ewan I'll see you on Monday morning.

Fiona I do like you.

Ewan goes through the tunnel.

Vari So. Now we wait.

Fiona Och, shut up.

Vari goes, singing 'Bye, Bye, Blackbird'. Fiona stays on the beach and joins in for two or three verses.

All right. I've made a mistake. I won't get pregnant. I won't get pregnant. I bet I won't. I bet I won't. Virgins don't often get pregnant first off. It'll be tonight. That'll be the end of it and I won't speak to him again. He can be at the bus stop all he likes, I won't so much as look at him. Stuck-up pig. Who does he think he is, with his great long legs and his manners? Stuff his manners. Stuff him. I mean, it takes two. He didn't have to. He could have said no. Stupid black PVC raincoat. He thinks he's great. He's not, he's not. I'll swim in the sea. I'll wash him all off me. He'll be nowhere. I'll wash him all out of me. He won't exist. He won't be in me. He'll be in his stupid piece of black plastic and nowhere else. I'll be clear. I'm so cold.

Morag Fiona. What are you doing?

Fiona Nothing.

Morag Are you all right?

Fiona I'm fine.

Morag Do you know what the time is?

Fiona Late.

Morag You shouldn't be on the rocks at this hour. You should have come straight home after the pictures. I've sat up waiting.

Fiona Come for a swim.

Morag What's the matter with you?

Fiona I feel like a swim.

Morag It's the middle of the night.

Fiona Best time.

Morag It's cold.

Fiona Keep your clothes on.

Morag All right.

Fiona You're kidding.

Morag In, under and out. Race you.

Fiona You're kidding.

Morag Race you. Come on.

Fiona You're mad. It's bloody freezing in there.

Morag It's your idea.

Fiona You're on.

Morag On your marks, get set, go.

   They rush in.

Oh, my God.

Fiona Jesus Christ.

Morag Beat you.

Fiona It's a draw.

Morag I got in first.

Fiona I was under first.

Morag Last one out's a cissy.

Fiona Ready, steady, go.

   They race out on to the rocks.

Jesus.

Morag Come here and give me a cuddle.

   They put their arms round each other.

What happened?

Fiona When?

Morag You were upset.

Fiona I'm bloody freezing.

Morag We'll have a mug of hot chocolate when we get in.

Fiona Me for the bath first.

Morag Was it wandering hands?

Fiona Yes.

Morag You just have to be firm.

Fiona I was.

Morag That's all right, then.

Fiona Mum . . .

Morag What?

Fiona Race you to the house.

Blackout.

SCENE 2

1983
The beach. The sun is shining.
Fiona is sitting with a towel round her shoulders. Vari is
on the travelling rug.

Vari Do you find it much changed?

Fiona It's the same.

Vari You're not looking. See round the corner. There's a nuclear power station.

Fiona Where?

Vari Breathe in. Go on. Through your nose. What do you smell?

Fiona Air.

Vari There you are, you see. No sewers. You can't smell the shit, can you?

Fiona Where is it? This nuclear power station.

Vari It's like a fairy palace when it's all lit up.

Fiona You like it.

Vari Away back there. The sun shines off the sea and the glass of the reactors. It's a jewel in the green trees.

Fiona Don't be daft.

Vari There's building dirt from the B reactor. That's begun now. Do you know what they're doing with the dirt? Do you?

Fiona Tell me.

Vari Land from the sea. They're reclaiming it. See, that's creative. That shows conscience. And the work isn't allowed to disturb the environment. On that site there's flowers and trees. That's considerate. They fixed the sewers.

Fiona You live round the corner from that.

Vari I'm not the only one.

Fiona Come on.

Vari Lots of people do.

Fiona For Christ's sake.

Vari It's clean. It's awful pretty. All those lights twinkling like stars in the black night.

Fiona Waste.

Vari My mother always said it doesn't matter what the house is like, it can be a midden as long as the bathroom's clean. Then you know the woman of the house hasn't been got by the Apathy. I mean this place. It was a shit bin. I've three children. Shit can kill. Dog shit. People shit. My children wouldn't have been allowed near this beach if the sewers hadn't been fixed. Because they might tire me out but I love them.

Fiona It wasn't as bad as that.

Vari Wasn't it?

Fiona How many reactors are there going to be?

Vari A, B and C. You haven't kids, what do you know? You were never a mother.

Fiona What was I then?

Vari Down the road the old coal-fired place belting its muck out. Remember? Wind off the sea, shit; wind from the West, smoke. It's shut down now. Breathing that stuff. You don't live here. I mean, having the baby, it was a hiccup for you. You dropped it, passed it on, gave it away. You know nothing. It had no effect on your life. You changed schools. You got to university. Look at you now. No responsibilities. What do you know? It was all taken care of for you.

Fiona I was fifteen.

Vari I'm thirty-two. Sometimes I feel fifty. You got away with it. Slender young thing. I hate you.

Fiona If there's an accident with the reactors your kids will suffer.

Vari See, you. You've changed. You've got thinner. Me, I'm always going to be lumpy. So I hate you. Your face is taut, you've got cheek-bones. You've got the make-up right in the corner of your eyes. That takes time. I haven't got time. You'll be a member of CND and some left-wing political group with militant affiliations and pacifist intent. You'll wear dungarees, speak harsh words of men and belong to a feminist encounter group where you look up your genitals with a mirror. I watch telly. Of course your blouses come from market stalls ten a penny but your shoes cost a packet. I know you. I've seen you on demonstrations on the telly. I haven't got time. I keep my hair short for it's less bother that way. I wear a pair of elastic panties from Marks and Spencer's to keep my tummy in and to stop my bum from shoogling. I play badminton once a week in the same church hall we had the youth club in when we were young and I promise myself I'll have a sauna in some health club and a weekend in London when my youngest is weaned. If Archie says I can. For he's got the money. I have acquired a major accomplishment. Compromise. Listen. This is what I chose. I'm happy till you march in with no bottom and a social conscience.

Fiona I'm sorry.

Vari What for? You can't help it any more than I can. But get it right, Fiona, get it right.

Vari wanders down and stands looking out to sea.

1966
The beach.

Fiona (*very quickly*) Last week, I was on the bus, upstairs. I was going to see Dorothy and this girl up the front, she started having a fit or something. Must have been the heat. There were lots of people there between her and me but they, none of them . . . I went over to her and did what I could. She was heavy. I'd heard about them biting through their tongues. Epileptics. It wasn't pretty. Me and this other bloke took her to the hospital. But I saw her first. He wouldn't have done anything if I hadn't. I didn't get to see Dorothy. Well? That's worth something, isn't it? God. Are you listening? I'm not trying to bribe you. It's plain economics. I mean, I've made a mistake. It was my fault and I was wrong. I take it all on me. OK. Now if you let it make me pregnant . . . God. Listen, will you. If I'm pregnant it'll ruin four people's lives. Five. Right? My

Mum'll be disappointed and her man'll walk out on her.
That's two. Are you with me, God? I'll not be very happy.
My Mother'll hate me for the rest of my life for what I've
done and that's not easy to live with. That's three. I'm still
counting, God. Ewan'll be in for it. Well, he can't avoid it.
I'm illegal and I've never been out with anybody else. Not
that nobody fancied me. I wouldn't like you to think I was
unpopular. Lots of people fancied me. My Mum said I had
to wait till I was sixteen. Then she relented just when
Ewan happened to be there. Poor old Ewan. That's four,
God, that's four. Then there's the baby. If it's there and if I
have it it's got no chance. It would be born in Scotland.
Still there, are you? I hate Scotland. I mean, look at me. If
I have an abortion the baby'll be dead so that'll be five
anyway.

Vari Who the hell are you talking to?

Fiona 'scuse me. Cover your ears.

Vari Eh?

Fiona Do it. This is private. Thank you. Sorry, God.
You'll see from the aforegoing that you really don't need
another soul in the world through me. You could let my
Mum have a miracle baby with her man. She's only forty-
two. It's still possible and she'd be really chuffed if you
would. So we'll regard that as settled, then. Thank you
very much for your attention. You can deal with
something else now. Amen.

Vari There's no God.

Fiona I know.

Vari What are you doing then?

Fiona You were listening.

Vari What do you expect? How are you feeling?

Fiona Fine, thanks. How are you?

Vari You know what I mean.

Fiona The fair on Saturday. Did you go? I stayed on the chairoplanes for half an hour. It cost me a fortune. I was sick when I got off.

Vari What for?

Fiona I thought I might shake it loose.

Vari You think it's there then?

Fiona I don't know.

Vari When are you due?

Fiona Next week.

Vari I can't stand the suspense. It's making me itchy.

Fiona Look. It's my Mum.

Morag is above.

Vari So what?

Fiona You're not to say anything.

Morag Dinner's ready.

Fiona Can Vari come? Will there be enough food?

Vari I've got my dinner waiting for me at home.

Morag My man'll be there.

Fiona That'll be nice. You're coming.

Vari Don't order me about.

Fiona Please.

Vari I'll have to phone my Mum.

Blackout.

SCENE 3

1966
The beach.
Fiona is alone on the beach in the sunshine.

Fiona Three old ladies with shopping bags. God. One
blind woman to the hairdresser's. That was a hard one. It
was right out of my way. How many stars do I get for
that? I mean, do you deal in stars as well as black marks?
God. Here's the biggie. I fixed it for my Mum to go with
her man. I don't want to be left. You've got to realize I've
made a big sacrifice. I've been completely unselfish. How
many people can come here and say that to you, God? I've
done something entirely for someone else. Are you
impressed? Are you? I've fixed it for my Mum to go to the
Trucial States with her man. His name's Robert, just so
you know. I'm going to go to Vari's. You really should do
something about her Mother. Talk about black marks. So
it's fixed. Were you around when I did it? It was at the
dinner table. He was there, Robert, and so was Vari. I
said, 'By the way. I think you two need to be alone
together for the start of your marriage. Why don't you
take your honeymoon on the Gulf? I'll be very happy to
stay with Vari and I hope you two'll be happy for you
have my blessing.' I did it just like that. Sort of formal and
casual at the same time. The right touch, I thought. Vari
giggled. My Mum. Did you see? My Mum lit up. I've
never seen her look like that. She's always had these
graven lines from her nose to her mouth. Way since I can
remember. They went. Daft, eh, God? Bet you weren't
looking. I've never seen anyone look happy like that. He,
Robert, looked more than a wee bit pleased too. I don't
want her to go. I'll have nobody it doesn't matter with. I
won't have somebody of my own. I'll have to write letters.
I hate writing letters. Still, I think it's worth it. Don't you,

71

God? They say I can go out for the school holidays. I'll like that fine. Listen to me, God. You've not to let those little fish meet the seed. Let them chase their own tails. Anything you like. Kill them off. Don't let them make a baby. God. God. Are you there? God. Come on. Och, damn you then.

Ewan comes down through the tunnel on to the rocks.

Ewan Hello.

Fiona Hello.

Ewan How have you been?

Fiona Fine.

Ewan I've not seen you at the bus stop.

Fiona I've been getting the 42.

Ewan I see.

Pause.

Fiona How have you been?

Ewan Very well, thank you.

Fiona And your studies?

Ewan Fine. What about you?

Fiona Prime university material.

Ewan That's good then.

Fiona Yes.

Pause.

You don't have to be polite because we've fucked.

Pause.

Ewan I hear your Mother's going away.

Fiona That's the idea.

Ewan When?

Fiona It'll be a couple of months yet.

Pause.

Did you know that the moment of conception can take place up to two days after a fuck? I mean, you don't just do it and boom you're pregnant. It can take up to two days of swimming. I wonder what I was doing when I conceived.

Ewan I don't . . .

Fiona I could have been having a piss at the time or playing netball. I've been playing a lot of netball and badminton and tennis. I've been swimming. Hockey's over but I've been playing volleyball. Two a side. It's a fast game. I've fallen over a lot. Look at this knee. It's had a terrible thumping. We won the school badminton tournament, me and my partner. We were rank outsiders. A hundred-to-one shot. I could have been playing badminton when I conceived. My O levels start next week.

Ewan Are you pregnant by me?

Fiona That was the idea.

Ewan Why?

Fiona I love you madly and I want to be your wife.

Ewan Will you marry me?

Fiona Very noble.

Ewan Well?

Fiona How old are you?

Ewan Seventeen next month.

Fiona I'm fifteen. I don't want to marry you. I don't want to marry anyone and I don't want to have a baby.

Ewan Don't you like me?

Fiona Not much. I'm sure you're a very nice person but you're not really my type.

Pause.

Ewan You're being honourable.

Fiona No.

Ewan You couldn't have done it with me if you hadn't loved me.

Fiona It was quite exciting.

Pause.

Ewan What are you going to do?

Fiona It's nothing to do with you.

Ewan It's my child.

Fiona You were the donor. That's all. You're not to tell anyone. I'm doing my O levels in peace.

Ewan Will you get rid of it?

Fiona Probably. Now go away.

He gets up to go.

Ewan. Do you love me?

Ewan I could get used to the idea.

Fiona If you didn't love me why did you do it? Promise you won't tell.

Ewan goes through the tunnel.

I wasn't christened. That's what's wrong, isn't it? I was a

74

lost soul to begin with. I'll get christened if you'll take it away. Do me a favour, will you, God. It's not my fault I wasn't christened. I feel sick all the time and I've got to get through my O levels. Churches make me cry. I'll believe in you if you'll take this away. I don't like it at all.

Vari enters.

Vari You're getting fat.

Fiona I know.

Vari You'll have to tell. Your Mum's going in a fortnight.

Fiona She's sold the house.

Vari You shouldn't have let her do that. What does it feel like?

Fiona Heavy. I'm tired all the time.

Vari Isn't it nice?

Fiona No.

Vari I think you're lucky. You'll never be alone again.

Morag comes through the tunnel.

Fiona Shut up. Jesus, that's stupid.

Morag I've bought so many things. Fiona, I bought you two dresses. I took a guess at the size. You're chubby these days but awful pretty. Take them back if you don't like them. Vari, I've bought you a jumper. You've a nice bust. It's a skinny rib. Here. It'll show you off. You mind with the boys now. Fiona, I've one for you too. You're getting a bust yourself. Think yourself lucky. I've done without all my life. That'll be your father's side of the family.

Vari You shouldn't have bought anything for me. Auntie Morag.

Morag Don't you like it?

Vari It's lovely. Thank you very much.

Morag Fiona?

Fiona It's smashing.

Morag I wish you both health to wear them.

Vari And happiness.

Morag You'll have that, all right. You're fair good girls.

Fiona OK, God. I'm not going to tell her. This is what I've decided. You're to back me up now, you hear. I'll do it on my own. After she's gone. After the O levels, I'll go down to London and get an abortion and don't you come it. You've left me no choice. I mean, it wasn't much to ask. She'll leave me money. She's bound to. Vari and me'll say we're going to visit friends. Kate Alex, her that had the restaurant, she moved to London. She'll back us. All you've got to do. Are you listening? Don't let me down this time. All you've got to do is not let me show till after she's gone and the O levels are past. I mean, chubby's all right but I don't want any bumps. Now listen to me. You've done nothing I've asked so far. Don't go trying anything off your own bat. I've taken the initiative. No bumps. Right? Right, God? Right?

Morag Fiona.

Fiona What?

Silence. Fiona and Morag look at each other.

Hey, God.

Silence.

76

1966
The beach.
Ewan is at the tunnel entrance. Fiona walks over to him.

Fiona You're a wee shit, aren't you?

Ewan I did it for the best.

Fiona What best? Who's best? What were you? Playing the fucking hero. Is that it?

Ewan I hardly think . . .

Fiona No, you don't, do you? You don't think. What did you think was gonnie happen? Come on. I'm interested. What did you think you'd accomplish with your blabbing mouth? What did you think? What did you think? I'm fucking fascinated to know.

Ewan I thought . . .

Fiona I can see you, standing there with your head bowed. Did you bow your wee head, Ewan, in all humility? Did you duck your wee fat bonce? Were your big bony knees shaking? Were you humble? 'I'm awfully sorry, Mrs McBridie, but your dear sweet daughter Fiona, of whom I'm awfully fond, I hope you'll forgive me but I stuck one up her and now she's in the family way.' Is that your style, Ewan? Is it? Did it go like that? Did I get it right? Answer me.

Ewan I think . . .

Fiona No, not you. Did you come the big man? Did you stand there tall, your proud head held high? Up on your high arse. 'I've done wrong, Mrs McBridie. Fiona's pregnant. I have no apologies to make. I'm prepared to marry her.' Was that it, Ewan? Or did you tell her her daughter's a whore? Did you sit her down with a nice wee drink? Did you bring her a bunch of flowers? Did you walk her round the garden? How did you tell her? Come on. Come on. Answer me. Cunt.

Ewan hits Fiona. Silence.

That's a mighty answer. There's a big man. Potent and virile. He can fuck a bint and he can swing his fists too.

Ewan It wasn't easy.

Fiona No.

Ewan I felt I had to.

Fiona Yes.

Ewan You couldn't go on alone.

Fiona What do you think I'm going to be now? I was getting on fine with my mother and she liked me. We were turning into good companions. What do you think you've done to that?

Ewan You're pregnant.

Fiona Congratulations.

Ewan Fiona.

Fiona Och, well.

Ewan I felt I had to.

Fiona Go away.

Ewan I . . .

Fiona Go away.

Ewan goes out. Fiona sits on the towel.

1983
The beach.

Morag We've had beautiful weather. We've been that

lucky with the weather. Of course, we were always tanned when we lived here. In the summer months. Now they're saying it's not good for you, the sun. I can't see that that's right. I mean too much of anything . . . Look at orange juice and that man. Or was it carrots that killed him? But that was plain silly. Sun. In this country. How can you get too much? And they made that pool with their own hands. Men. They brought their wee tools and they chiselled it out in the hot days. Drinking their beer and telling their dirty jokes. Well, they would, wouldn't they? Men do. They built it to save their feet on the hot rocks. Great soft things. Fancy going to all that trouble to save a 15-yard walk. They never brought their wives. Of course, that was when I was wee. When I think of it now, I think they must have been the unemployed. They were here an awful lot. Nice men they were too. They got raucous as the day went on with the beer and then I wasn't allowed near the beach. The storms there were. Summer and winter. You'd see the spray coming right up over the roofs of the houses. I used to stand in the mouth of the tunnel. I used to dare the waves to come and get me. I'd run forward and I'd run back. My Mum'd leather me for being wet when I got in. It was worth it. Once I asked her for a raincoat. A special present for my birthday. A real waterproof. I wanted it to keep me dry from the spray. She bought it for me. It was a real one. Kept me snug and dry. When I got in my Mum belted me across the face. She had a hard hand. Then she chased me round the house with the bread knife. For getting the raincoat wet. She was angry. I feel so disappointed.

Fiona We could have gone to the Lakes for Christ's sake.

Morag I'll love you whatever you do. You know that. I've loved you through it all.

Fiona Don't be stupid.

Morag You're my daughter.

Fiona If I tortured, if I murdered, you'd love me then?

Morag You're my flesh and blood.

Fiona It means nothing. (*She clicks her fingers.*) It means *that*. It's an insult, Mother.

Morag I stood by you.

Fiona Is that why we've come here?

Morag I wanted to talk. I couldn't talk to you. You're a queer lass but I love you.

Fiona Did it ever occur to you, you had a choice?

Morag What?

Fiona You had a choice. Did you know that? Did you know you had a choice?

Morag Suppose I did?

Fiona Oh, Jesus.

Morag Further and further away from me. The years pass. Each day. Vegetarian food. Symphonies. You put up barriers and I'm . . . We never had a symphony in the house. There was no need. I mean, I had other things . . . Time was, I'd go out, I'd buy you something. Impulse. I'd be in a shop. Some wee thing. You'd like it. I'd know you'd like it. Now. I wanted to talk to you. Books. I don't like Dickens. I never did. I like Georgette Heyer and I like the television. I'm very fond of the television. Your flat. You've not got an ashtray in your flat. Not a single one.

Fiona I don't smoke.

Morag Of course you don't smoke. Live and let live. I've always said that. I hold to that. You have men and I say

80

nothing though I'd like it if you'd talk to me. For years. I held down a good job.

Fiona I know you did.

Morag I'm not a stupid woman.

Fiona I never said . . .

Morag Choice, choice, choice. Yes, yes. I knew there was a choice. Let me find the right word. I like to have the right word. The exact right word. Culpable. You and me. See now. I know you're not all to blame. I'm culpable. Not the going away.

Fiona What then?

Morag I mean, I met a man and I loved him. I met a man and I was glad he wanted me. Do you see? I wanted to go away with him. So what's more natural than that? Come on.

Fiona I told you to . . .

Morag See me now. Look. I knew what I'd become. I made a break for something. OK. When he came to me, Ewan. When he came to me and told me.

Fiona Mum, this is . . .

Morag You listen. 'Mrs McBridie, Fiona's going to have a child. It's my child. I'm sorry, Mrs McBridie.' Oh, he was polite. I liked him. Poor wee fella. I liked him fine.

Fiona He was . . .

Morag Now listen to me. I knew I had a choice. Listen. My daughter had not come to me. Do you understand that? My daughter was not asking for my help. I could see her point. Listen. I had a choice. What if I left her enough money and I went away? Nothing mentioned between us. I knew you'd not have that child. Then you might say we'd survive, you and me. Out of the question. Fifteen and pregnant. Of course I couldn't let you alone. So. You told Ewan. So. Here we both are. Here we are.

Pause.

I expect you'd like an ice-cream cone. I'll walk up the prom a bit. My last walk of this holiday. I don't expect you ever will talk to me. Would you like a double 99 with raspberry sauce? That's what I'm having. My own wee treat. Will you join me? You've got to do something daft on a last day.

Fiona That would be lovely.

Morag Don't if you'd rather not.

Fiona Bunny rabbit's ears. A double 99.

Fiona You'll join me then?

Fiona Yes.

Morag After all, it's not meat.

Fiona I'll join you.

Morag That's good then. That's very good.

She goes off up the tunnel. Vari's voice comes from beside the swimming pool.

Vari Your Mother's alive. They all are, that generation. My Mother's the same. She's an old cow but she's zinging with it. Life. Me, sometimes I get this awful dizzy feeling. I'm standing there. I'm doing something. I don't know what day of the week it is. I panic. I mean, I really don't know. I hang on to myself. If I don't I'll fall down. I put my arms round myself and hug tight. I hug very tight. I look out the window to see what the weather's like. See, I don't know where I am in the year. And I'm dizzy. I lean my back to the sink. I check the big tree outside the

window. If it's got leaves. I look down at my clothes.
What's the month? What month is it? What year is it?
How many children have I got? Am I pregnant now? Have
I just given birth? I don't know. I don't know. And then it
comes to me. It's Wednesday. It's October. It's Sunday. It's
April. It's all the same and I turn back to the sink. I wash
the nappies by hand. I've got a washing machine, don't
you worry. One of the ones that does it all. You know,
dries as well. I've a dish-washer too. I wash the nappies by
hand. They're cleaner that way. Not that I care. I don't
care, but you have to have something to talk about at
mothers' mornings. Do something queer. Marks you out.

Fiona My Mother cares passionately about everything.
Life and a ham sandwich. It all has the same importance.
Not a touch of the Apathy. God? Do you still live here or
have you moved on? Hung up your omniscience and
retired the Recording Angel? Would it be too much to ask,
I'd like to be let alone?

Morag comes through the tunnel with the ice-creams.

Morag Bunny rabbit's ears. The raspberry sauce is
running down my hands. Here, take it quick, Fiona. I'd
have brought you one, Vari, if I'd known. Here, have one
of my ears.

Vari Thank you, Auntie Morag.

Morag I've some whisky in my bag. Reach me it over. Our
last day. You'll drink with us, the Parting Glass. Eat your
ice-cream, Fiona. A wee bit of what you fancy.

*She one-handedly arranges glasses and begins to
unscrew the bottle as the lights fade down.*

WHEN WE WERE WOMEN

Characters

Maggie A woman of forty-five
Isla Her daughter
Alec Isla's father
Mackenzie A Chief Petty Officer in the Royal Navy
Cath A woman

The action takes place in Scotland at the time of the
Second World War.

When We Were Women was first performed at the
Cottesloe Theatre, London, in September 1988. The cast
was as follows:

Maggie Mary Macleod
Isla Rebecca Pidgeon
Alec Henry Stamper
Mackenzie Ewan Stewart
Cath/Woman Jan Shand

Directed by John Burgess
Designed by Alison Chitty
Lighting by Ian Dewar
Choreographed by Dorothy Max Prior

Act One

SCENE I

1944
The back living room, cosy, with a fire and a table and
fruit. A mirror over the fireplace. A black fender. It's a
room of spit and polish. In the front room there's a full-
sized billiards table. This is not a poor house. It's red
sandstone and it's big. Nevertheless, its atmosphere is
working class. **Maggie** *is dotting around with her coat on*
over her apron. **Alec**'s *at the fire.* **Isla** *is at the table reading*
a magazine.

Maggie You could help me, the one or the other of you.
The black one. Where is it? Get you up off your great
backside. Ma black caiddie. You. You. Sittin' there.

Isla Well?

Maggie Where is it then?

Isla You don't need it.

Maggie I'm not goin' up that road wi' ma bare head.
You're sittin' on it. That's where it is alright.

Isla I am not.

Maggie Under your bahoochey. That's where it is.

Isla I'm not sitting on it.

Maggie Don't tell me. I've the Police Station to walk by.
You're sittin' on it.

Isla You'll not be clapped in irons for the lack of a hat.

Maggie Sittin' there.

89

Isla Will you?

Alec Get up will you.

Isla Eh?

Alec Can you no just stand up?

Isla If I was sittin' on a hat I'd know. Wouldn't I. I'm not in my dotage.

Maggie And I am I suppose.

Alec Hod yer noise.

Maggie I've had about enough of you.

Alec Satisfy your Mother.

Maggie Well then.

Isla By your foot.

Maggie Eh?

Isla Your foot.

They look, the two of them, Alec and Maggie.

Maggie Och. Could you no have said?

Alec sniggers.

Alec God's streuth.

Maggie You'll not laugh at me. Don't you laugh at me.

Alec Och, yer aye goin' off half-cock woman. (*He starts to cough.*)

Maggie Would you listen to him. (*She pours him a whisky.*)

Isla Don't give him that.

Maggie A poor cold that's what he's got.

Isla Let him be.

Maggie Kills the germs.

Isla Pouring that down his throat.

Alec That stuff. It'll no kill anything that stuff.

Maggie My own house. My own husband. You'll not tell me how to look after my own man.

Alec Have its work cut out for it this stuff.

Maggie You'll not tell me what to do.

Alec Away. Away wi' you.

Maggie I've done better than you my girl an' that's a fact.

Alec The pair of you. I'll have some generosity between you. The both of you. Do you hear me now? Do you? (*He pours ginger beer into the whisky.*)

Maggie A new hat, that's what I could do wi', A brand new caiddie. (*She bangs the hat against her leg.*)

Alec Bye-bye foam. Wee slip of a thing you were. Sittin' at ma knee. Bye-bye foam. All those years ago.

Maggie Duntin' it's no goin' tae bring it back into the fashion. All the duntin' it's had. Duntin' an' duntin'. All the duntin' in the world'll no save this hat.

Alec Bye-bye foam. The years pass. Aye they do. They do that.

Maggie Died long ago this hat. (*Jams it on her head.*)

Alec Bye-bye.

Maggie Sittin' there.

Isla The tea.

Maggie Do I no look a sight.

Isla It'll be made for you to come back to.

Maggie Great hummock on yer front. Sittin' there.

Alec Bye-bye foam.

Maggie goes.

Bye, bye, bye. (*He pours another glass of whisky.*) Here. Come here. (*He holds it out to Isla.*)

Isla You never used to drink this early.

Alec I'm no drinking now.

Isla What do you call this?

Alec I signed the pledge for you. Do you mind? Eh?

Isla Yes.

Alec The Band of Hope.

Isla No that you . . .

Alec Aye the years pass. I've always liked a good glass of whisky. Here. Come on. What do you think. D'you think I'd ruin a good glass of whisky wi' ginger beer. Would I commit that sacrilege. I respect him up there, the good God in his Heaven. What would I do. Would I ruin it. The greatest of his gifts to man. Come on. Come here. Would I? Would I do that?

Isla drinks.

Water. She's been waterin' it for years. Water an' a wee bit tea. We've had that same bottle since the boys went. I've no had a decent glass . . . no in this house. She's a grand woman your Mother . . . Thinks I don't know. She canny have a large regard for my intelligence if she thinks I don't know. A grand woman. I'm damned if I don't think she laces it mind. Syrup of figs . . . Every so often I get this wee hint of a taste . . . That's what I think she laces it wi'.

Syrup of figs. Your Mother's answer tae every damn thing that is. A cold in the heid tae a bereavement. She's a great woman. (*He puts ginger beer in her glass.*) This'll see you right. Eh? Bye-bye. Bye-bye foam.

1943
The fire sparks.
There's a street and a man walking up it. No street lights.
An edge of light from one window where the blackout
doesn't fit. The sound of bombs falling here and there.
Flashes of light. Firelight. One loud bang. **Mackenzie** *hits*
the deck in the middle of the road. He's in full uniform,
with a raincoat over his arm. Quiet. Mackenzie starts to
crawl up the road on his belly.

Mackenzie I'll get there if it damn well kills me. Eh God. If you see what I've got waitin' for me you'd no send your bombers in.

> Our Father which art in Heaven
> I am a sinner
> Hallowed be thy name.
> A terrible sinner.
> Thy kingdom come.
> I humbly ask.
> Thy will be done.

Do not snuff me out. Me. God. Not me. I mean God. You're a man. God. We're men together God. You and me. The pleasures of the flesh eh. Soft flesh. Wrap you round. I bet you've had your fling God. In your time. You've got to admit it. You were a one. Eh? Eh? And now, eh? Stuck up there in your nice heaven what have you got left. A pile of angels. There's no a lot you can do wi' an angel. I mean when it comes right down to it. God. Looking that's all you've got left. You're a bit of a voyeur.

93

Bang.

Mother Eve see to me. Mother Mary beloved of God hold me to thy bosom.

Bang.

Perfumed skin. Powder. Red, red lips. Succour me.

Bang.

We're no gettin' very far here are we now. I mean look at me. A more foolish . . . Let me go. Come on. You let me go an' I'll sin some more for your amusement God. Not bad sins when you come right down to it. Wee sins in a minor key. When you consider what could be done. There's a lot worse sinners than me . . . Aw, come on, man . . . There's no bloody dignity in crawlin' along a wet road on your belly.

Bang.

Give us this day our daily bread.

That's it. That's yer lot. I canny remember the rest of your prayer God. God. Lord. Lord God. Let me off the rest of your prayer. Give me one more day to breathe your crisp clean air.

Bang. He covers his head. Silence. The sound of crying. He lifts his head.

You made me. You've got me. Take me or leave me as I am. God. God.

Isla is sitting by a lamp post. Mackenzie crawls across the road to her.

Mackenzie What the hell.

Isla I can't see in the dark.

Mackenzie What are you doing out?

Isla My torch is broken.

Mackenzie There's bombs falling from the sky.

Isla I've bumped my head.

The all-clear sounds. Mackenzie salutes the heavens.

Mackenzie Here. Give it here.

Isla What.

Mackenzie Give me the torch.

Isla I walked into a lamp post.

Mackenzie That was smart.

Isla You're not very sympathetic. My head's sore.

Mackenzie shakes the torch.

My face is all wet.

The beam comes on.

Am I bleeding.

Mackenzie takes out a handkerchief and wipes her face.

Is that clean?

Mackenzie looks at her.

Well?

Mackenzie You've a cut over your eye.

Isla Do I look awful?

Mackenzie What were you out for?

Isla None of your business.

Mackenzie Manners. Manners.

Isla Ow.

Mackenzie Sorry.

Isla I'm alright.

Mackenzie What was so important?

Isla I had a bet on.

Mackenzie You'll need stitches in that.

Isla No one's stitching me. I know you.

Mackenzie My God. My God. Covered in blood. It's the Spanish Princess.

Isla Eh?

Mackenzie I know you.

Isla Say that again.

Mackenzie What?

Isla That. What you called me.

Mackenzie Spanish Princess.

Isla That's nice.

Mackenzie You. You water the beans in that canteen.

Isla I do not.

Mackenzie Aye you do.

Isla I don't.

Mackenzie Think you can stand?

Isla I can stand.

Mackenzie Here.

He holds out his hand. She doesn't take it.

Isla I'm fine.

Mackenzie Are you now?

Isla I do not water the beans.

Mackenzie Where's your hat?

Isla I haven't got one.

Mackenzie You canny be a lady if you havenie got a hat.

Someone lifts the blackout blind behind them. A shaft of light streams out. A voice shouts, 'Aileen'. The light goes out. A figure stands at an open window. Mackenzie grabs Isla's elbow. He takes her into the shadow.

No that I'm fond of ladies mind.

Isla Are you not.

Mackenzie That's no where my heart lies.

Isla shakes free of him. She tries to walk away. She stumbles. He steadies her.

Isla I'm alright.

Mackenzie I'll see you home.

Isla You will not.

Mackenzie My old Gran said always to take care of damsels in distress.

Isla My Gran said 'Keep your haund on your Ha'penny.'

Mackenzie Is that right?

Isla I know you. You with your raincoat. You think you're God's gift you do. The lot of you. Don't think I don't know you.

Mackenzie Here.

He gives her the torch. She walks away. The torch goes out.

97

Isla Oh. Oh damn. (*Takes another couple of steps.*) It's no me. The beans. They come like that. The beans. (*Shakes the torch. It doesn't come on.*) I can't see in the dark. (*Shakes the torch. It doesn't come on.*) Please.

Mackenzie What was the bet?

Isla I'm not telling you.

Mackenzie Night. Night.

Isla Come here.

Mackenzie Well?

Isla I want you to take me . . .

Mackenzie Night. Night.

Isla Please.

Mackenzie The bet.

Isla Half a pint of gin.

Mackenzie Eh?

Isla Straight down.

Mackenzie Down what. Down where.

Isla Well it wouldnie be down the stank would it?

Mackenzie You were gonnie drink a half-pint of gin.

Isla So what?

Mackenzie A whole half-pint.

Isla Down in one an' stay standin' up.

Mackenzie I'll see you home.

Isla I don't want to go home.

Mackenzie Home.

Isla No.

Mackenzie What are you? Are you daft? I mean I like alcohol. I'm no sayin' I don't like alcohol. Home.

Isla I'm a grown woman.

Mackenzie Are you now?

Isla I can do what I like.

Mackenzie You treat alcohol wi' respect. Look at you. You canny stand up right. I'll get you to your own home if I have to carry you there. And don't think I can't. I've carried heavier than you. (*He holds out his arm.*)

Isla I think I'd be safer wi' the gin.

Mackenzie I'll tell you something.

Isla What?

Mackenzie Right at this very moment you're no that appealing. I mean, when yer cleaned up a bit you might just pass muster. But right now, right now . . .

She takes his arm. They walk.

Spanish Princess. For your hair an' your hips an' your dark, dark eyes and the way you look at me and your hands wi' their great long fingers an' their red, red nails an' your shoulders an' your shoes an' your white, white socks. See they socks God. Women in white socks God. My God. We're all poor sinners in this vale of tears.

1944
In the room. Alec is sweeping at the rug with the brush and shovel from beside the fire. Isla's in the kitchen getting water.

Alec She'll smell it. That's what she'll do. Smell of burning wool. Hangs about. Open up the windaes will you. Wee pit holes in the rug. 'You should have had the fire-guard on.' I'm for it Isla. 'What did you not have the fire-guard on for?' She'll do me. 'You wi' your great feet. That's my good rug.' Pungent. That's what it is, burning wool. There's no getting away from it. Pungent smell that is.

Isla It's your rug too.

Alec I'll go into the works.

Isla comes in with a bowl of water, a bar of soap and a cloth.

She'll know. She'll know if it's wet.

Isla You can't help a coal fire sparking.

Alec That's what it's there for. The guard.

Isla You're scared of her.

Alec I've lived with your Mother for thirty years.

Isla Well then.

Alec I've learnt respect.

Isla For goodness sake.

Alec Your Mother's got a tongue on her.

Isla Dad.

Alec I've spent my life dodging your Mother's tongue.

Isla Pa Pa.

Alec I've not heard that . . . Pa Pa.

Isla scrubs at the rug.

You learn respect . . . Pa Pa. Not since you were a wee girl. (*He gets his collar and tie. His studs.*) Pa Pa. I'm away into ma work.

Isla Pa Pa.

Alec Aye.

Isla Look at me. (*She stands up.*) You've not looked at me. Not since I came home.

Alec My wee girl.

Isla Not so very wee.

Alec You'll always be that to me. My bonnie lassie.

Isla Look at me.

  He looks.

Alec Aye.

Isla I'm . . .

Alec What is it I'm to look at?

Isla Pa Pa.

Alec I can see you. I can see you.

Isla I'll clean the rug.

Alec Aye.

Isla I could . . .

Alec Aye.

Isla I could drive you in.

Alec Auntie Mac. D'you mind yer Auntie Mac? (*Puts his tie pin in.*) Always askin' for you yer Auntie Mac. Round an' round the place wi' her buckets an' her brooms. Never changes. (*Cuff links.*) Your Mother worries about the boys. She's a lot on her mind, your Mother. 'How is she then?' says Auntie Mac. Always the same. 'Does she mind the sugar mice? Your wee dark girl.' Auntie Mac never recovered from the day they pulled down the

Gorbals Cross. I'll go in by myself. I'll drive mysel' in.

Isla Pa Pa.

Alec You mind you've got that rug pristine by the time she comes back. Save your old Dad's hide eh?

Puts his jacket on. Twists and turns at the mirror.

How's that? How's that? Eh? See me when I was young. Cock of the walk when I was young.

Isla Pa Pa.

Alec Cock of the walk me.

Isla The Duke they called you when you were young.

Alec Aye an' then they called me the dirty Duke but we'll no dwell on that. My own wee girl. (*And he leaves her.*)

1943
Mackenzie lights a lighter. He's waiting near a cinema queue, raincoat draped upon his arm.

Mackenzie Girls (*He lights his cigarette.*) Girls. God. Girls. Rita. Flora. Annie. Annie. Oh my Great good God. No, no. That's it. That's alright. Annie's on someone's arm. Thank you God. Jack. Right you are then. Jack. Annie's with Jack. For a moment there . . . Eh God? Thank you. God. Bless Jack. Keep him safe from all harm. God. Hey God do you see what I see. Mary standin' there. Hey now you've let something slip. You're not taking care of me. Mary standin' there on her own. All, all alone. Hairy Mary in the cinema queue. Come on God. Come on. Come on. Is that fair. That standin' there. Is that fair to a man.

Isla links arms with him.

Oh! (*He pats all his pockets.*)

Isla What?

Mackenzie Wallet.

Isla What?

Mackenzie Wait.

Isla Why?

Mackenzie No.

Isla What?

Mackenzie No wallet.

Isla No?

Mackenzie Come on.

Isla Where are we going.

Mackenzie For a walk.

Isla We are not.

Mackenzie No wallet.

Isla I'm not goin' for any walk. I want to see that.

Mackenzie No money.

Isla I'll pay.

Mackenzie I'll have no woman pay for me.

Isla I want to see the film.

Mackenzie Want doesn't get. (*He walks off, away from the cinema queue.*) I'm not that sort of man.

Isla What sort?

Mackenzie Eh?

Isla What sort's that sort?

Mackenzie You're half daft you are.

Isla What sort of man are you?

Mackenzie Cut it out.

Isla I'll slip you the money. No one'll see.

Mackenzie No.

Isla I want to see the film. I've the money here. What's wrong with me paying? You can give me it back if you're so . . . The queue's almost gone. I want to see this film. The queue's gone in. It's Clark Gable in there.

Mackenzie Ah.

Isla What?

Mackenzie The very thing. (*He pats his back pocket.*)

Isla What?

Mackenzie Nestled in here. Snug. Safe and sound. Didn't look there. Never thought. I don't keep my wallet there. Pick pockets. Spoils the line of a pair of trousers.

Isla You've got it.

Mackenzie Daft eh.

Isla Have you got a cigarette?

Mackenzie We'll miss the film.

> *Isla puts her hand into Mackenzie's inside jacket pocket. Finds his cigarette case and with it his wallet. She pulls them both out. Tosses the wallet to Mackenzie.*

Fancy that.

Isla See. Mary. Mary Stuart.

Mackenzie Clark Gable's in there.

Isla Stuart with a 'u'. Royal Stuart. Well of course Mary's a Royal Stuart. Mary. 'My family's always believed we were by blows of the kings.' Nose in the air. Used to show her knickers to the boys round the back of the synagogue. 'Wrong side of the blanket.' See. I know. I know you. Only ever showed her knickers. Then. I know you're not the clean potato. (*She reads the cigarette case.*) 'To Mackenzie. All my love Rita.' (*Takes a cigarette.*)

Mackenzie I don't like to see a woman smoke in the street.

Isla 'From Cath.' (*On the lighter.*)

Mackenzie Not my woman.

Isla I'm not yours. I belong to my own self. Don't you forget it. (*She lights the cigarette.*)

Who's Cath?

Silence.

See. I'm not the first woman in your life. Not by a long chalk. I know. But I'm telling you this. I'll make damn sure I'm the last. See that raincoat. You can stop carrying that raincoat. You'll not get me on that raincoat.

Blackout.

SCENE 2

1944
Maggie's walking up to the back door. She's carrying two heavy shopping bags. Her handbag's under her arm.

Maggie Feel the smell of that. All the way down the lane that's coming. Mrs Paterson'll smell that. Down at number four she'll smell that. The old ladies'll smell that. That's potatoes burning. That's onions burning. That's my good pot. My big pot. (*She gets in the back door, sets everything down. Rushes over to the stove. Grabs the pot, the handle's hot. Lifts up the corner of her coat. Uses that to pick up the pot. Rushes over to the sink with it.*) What is it that we're having to wur tea tonight. Is it bread we're having. If that's what we're having, that's all we're having. Right down the road I smelt that. What is it? What is it? Is it no enough . . . Do you want them all to know? Showing off your troubles. The waste. We're no so well off that we can afford to ruin good food. Sending your troubles to waft off down the street. Letting them all know. The stink of your troubles. You canny even set a pan of potatoes to boil. Och away an' stop yer greeting. (*She turns on the light.*) What're you sittin' in the dark for? There's dark enough in this world. Greetin' an' greetin'. Where's your pride? Have you no pride? Come on now. Come on. Look at your face. You'll ruin your face. (*She goes over to the table. She wipes the tears off Isla's face with her hand.*) You bathe your eyes in cold water before they all swell up. You're no the only one wi' troubles in this world. We've all got wur troubles. You're no even the only woman wi' a wain in her belly. You're my daughter an' you'll walk through this wi' your head up. I'm telling you. Och would you look at these hands . . . See these hands. Out in the garden wi' these hands I used to make mud pies when I was a wee wain. Same hands. Same hands. I'm a wain yet. Inside. We're all of us wains.

Isla 'Keep yer haund on your Ha'penny.' That's what Gran used to say.

Maggie Aye that's your Gran. That's yer Gran alright. Pity you didn't take her advice.

Isla I'm a married woman.

Maggie You. You're no more married than fly in the air. (*She puts the messages on the table.*)

Isla How much did you pay her?

Maggie If it'll no be too much strain you can give me a hand.

Isla doesn't move. Maggie begins to unpack.

Isla You're taking advantage of her.

Maggie Hold your tongue.

Isla She could go to prison for this.

Maggie I've more than you to take care of. I'll see my children right.

Isla My Father lets you do this.

Maggie There's more than me at it. I'll not see my children short.

Isla Sixpence. Is that what you give her? Come on. Do you give her sixpence? A nice shiny new sixpence. To herself. Maggie. Maggie. Is that what you give her?

Maggie You'll call me Mother.

Isla Ninepence. Is that it? Maggie. Is that her price?

Maggie You'll not address me by my given name.

Isla Is it more? Wee Jeannie down at Murray's. Does she come dearer than that. Does it cost you a shilling to get wee Jeannie to bend down behind that counter on a Thursday afternoon. You and all the others. Half-day closing. All of you. How much does she get wee soft Jeannie, to bring out the cheese and the butter an' the bacon an' the jam. Mother. What do you give her?

Maggie You in your righteousness. What do you know about me?

Isla The king's shilling.

Maggie I've my big son in a prisoner-of-war camp. Don't you talk to me.

Pause.

It's not for myself I'm doing this.

Isla And chocolate. You've got chocolate.

Maggie That was for you.

Pause.

She gets a good half-crown. Half a crown tae 'ersel'.

Isla That'll see her fine when she's in gaol. That'll see her right an' fine.

Maggie See what she's got put by. I'd like to have what she's got put by. Would I not. Come on hen. My wee hen. Here. (*She pushes the chocolate towards her.*) This stuff. It's all put by for the rich. I'm no depriving any other body. Our boys wouldn't get this, so they wouldn't. It's reserved. To keep 'Them' going. The Hoi Poloi. Why should I no get some. Rich men's cheeses. You talk about risk. I take a risk. Where's the harm. What harm is there. And eggs. I've got eggs. (*She takes the wrappings off a corner of the chocolate.*) A wee taste. A wee edge. There's iron in that. Feel the smell of that. You've got to take care of yoursel' for the sake of the wain that's in you . . . A wee piece of that. That'll take the burning from the back of your throat. That'll clear the tears away. (*Beat.*) Big brown eggs. (*Beat.*) It's a long time since you've had chocolate. (*Beat.*) Double yolks they'll have in they eggs. I'll warrant you that. (*Beat.*) A bit of chocolate. Do you good. Make you smile. Make you smile. Do you good. (*Beat.*) We'll keep an egg or two for wursels. We'll not give them all away. (*Beat.*) I like to see you smile. (*Beat.*) You see what I'll make you. (*Beat.*) Great yellow eggs we'll have an' a bit bacon to us. (*Beat.*) You'll have it made to you. On a tray.

On yer knees. At the fire. An' a bit of toast that you can douk in. All cut in soldiers. My hen. My wee hen. A bit chocolate. Is that not enough to make you salivate. A nice bit chocolate.

Isla leaves the kitchen.

Hen. My wee hen. Isla.

1943

Mackenzie Isla. (*Beat.*) You can't do it. You can not do it. (*Beat.*) There's a measure of stupidity coursing with the blood through the veins of a woman's body. (*Beat.*) Isla. (*Beat.*) There's a pigheadedness. (*Beat.*) Isla. (*Beat.*) Sheer pigheadedness. (*Beat.*) Isla. Will you listen to me. I know alcohol. Don't talk to me about alcohol. (*Beat.*) There's a bloody mindedness. (*Beat.*) I've seen men clutching at the chairs to stop them walking round the room. Grown men wi' blankets over their heads for fear of the beasties in the dark. That's alcohol. Isla. (*Beat.*) Come on now. Come you here to me now.

Isla is standing in an edge of light, holding half a pint of gin.

Don't be daft Isla. Pour it away.

Isla laughs. Mackenzie walks towards her.

Come on now. Come on now. There's no other body here. Pour it out.

Isla Mackenzie.

Mackenzie Pour it away now.

Isla Do you love me Mackenzie?

There's laughter from behind one of the windows. A radio goes on. There's dance music.

Mackenzie Don't be so damn silly.

Isla Mackenzie.

Mackenzie Put that drink down.

Isla Do you love me?

Mackenzie You'll not drink that.

Isla Mackenzie. (*She drinks.*)

Mackenzie No.

She drinks it down.

Oh my God.

Isla See. (*Beat.*) Didn't feel a thing. (*She passes straight out.*)

Mackenzie Dear God. Good God. Great God. (*He takes her pulse.*) Strange things happen in a war. I have to lift her. I have to carry her. Sweet body. Good body. Come on my Spanish Princess. You canny stay here.

He gets her arm round his neck. A voice shouts out from behind the blind with the bleeding light: 'Can you no fix this blind?' Someone fiddles with the blind. Cuts the light out.

I am a sinner.

The arm flops down.

Anybody could be lookin' here Isla.

He puts it back.

I am an evil man.

The arm flops down.

Spyin' out.

He puts the arm back.

A petty man.

He tries to take the weight. He can't.

My God. Will you pull yoursel' together Isla.

The arm flops down.

Come on now God. Will you give us a hand here. I mean, no shenanigans. I promise no shenanigans.

He gets the arm round his neck. It stays.

Right. Right. All right and tight.

He heaves her up.

Right. So far so good. Right. I know what you're thinkin'. I'm gonnie marry this woman . What's wrong with that? What the Hell's wrong wi' that?

In a light at a bus stop. In the far off distance, a woman (who looks like **Cath***) in a hat and raincoat, a suitcase at her side. Mackenzie looks.*

Nemesis. Eh God. Creeping up on me. I'm going to marry her. And why not? There's a war on. I'm going to marry her. Do you hear me? What the bloody Hell's wrong wi' that? (*He walks with Isla in his arms.*)

1944
Maggie (*yelling up the stairs from the door of the back living room*) Murray's. They make their fair whack out of it. It's a service they're providing an' don't they know it. Don't they charge enough. I've debts. I've bills coming in. What your Faither'll no do to me . . . I've not even got a good hat to my head. Where's the harm? Damn you, Isla, you'll not do this to me. Wee Jeannie's family'll not go short. Isla. What do you think? D'you think they go short? I'm not the only one at it. It's a social gathering up there of

a Thursday afternoon. You'd be surprised who I see up there. I'll not tell you who I see up there of a Thursday afternoon. I'll not tell you who's in that queue. Even a minister has to keep his strength up. For the preaching. God's work. Where's the harm? A wee bit lightness. A wee bit bacon. Is it no dark enough? I've your sister to think about. I've her children to think about. I've Moira. I've Ina. I'll not see them short. And the boys. The good God keep them and bless them and send them home. If they come home . . . Oh my God. My dear God. When they come home. I've the boys to think about. And you. I'll think about you. Though you're the bane of my life I'll think about you Isla. Isla.

Blackout.

SCENE 3

1943
When Isla comes to, she's lying on the raincoat. Mackenzie is kneeling beside her. There's a radio on in the background. It's a talk programme.

Isla Oh God.

Mackenzie Quiet.

Isla What have you done?

Mackenzie You passed out.

Isla You've taken advantage of me.

Mackenzie Eh?

Isla I'm lying on it.

Mackenzie What?

Isla This thing.

Mackenzie That's my raincoat.

Isla There you are then.

Mackenzie Eh?

Isla What have you done?

Mackenzie Eh?

Isla Well?

Mackenzie Well what?

Isla Have you?

Mackenzie Have I what?

Isla You know.

Mackenzie I don't.

Isla Have you?

Mackenzie I have not.

Isla You have.

Mackenzie I have not.

Isla You're despicable.

Mackenzie I haven't touched you.

Isla Have you not.

Mackenzie No.

Isla I don't believe you.

Mackenzie You should know.

Isla I wasn't going to end up here. No like the others. All that long line of all they others.

Mackenzie No that many.

Isla What am I going to do?

Mackenzie Yer alright.

Isla Am I?

Mackenzie For God's sake it's not that bloody appealing making love to a sack of potatoes.

Isla I feel terrible.

Mackenzie That's your own damn fault.

Isla I'm goin' to be sick.

Mackenzie No on my raincoat.

Isla Serve you right if I am.

Mackenzie I haven't done anything.

Isla Where am I?

Mackenzie Down the back lane.

Isla leaps up.

Isla Are you daft? They'll all can see.

Mackenzie I'm due back.

Someone turns the tuner on the radio then switches it off. Silence.

Isla What do I look like?

Mackenzie You'll do.

She pinches her cheeks and bites her lips.

You could have killed yoursel'.

Isla You care do you?

Mackenzie What do you damn well think?

Isla I'm just that wee bit shaky. Will you give me your arm.

She walks off to her own back door. It's open. There's a dull light coming out.

Well then.

Mackenzie Aye.

Isla What?

Mackenzie I'll say . . .

Isla What?

Mackenzie Well . . .

Isla Goodnight.

Mackenzie What?

Isla You'll say . . .

Mackenzie Goodnight?

Isla Right then. (*She turns to go.*)

Mackenzie Isla.

Isla Oh for goodness sake.

Mackenzie What?

Isla You can kiss me.

Mackenzie What?

Isla That's what you want isn't it?

Mackenzie Yes.

Isla Well then.

Mackenzie What?

Isla Come on.

Mackenzie Thank you.

A kiss. Chaste. A peck.

Isla What was so hard about that?

Mackenzie What?

Isla Goodnight. (*She turns to go.*)

Mackenzie No.

He grabs her hand, pulls her, whisks her round and down, across, round, running until they stop, kneeling in the light round the crack of a blackout window blind.

I, Howard . . .

He behind her. She kneeling in front of him. He cupping her hands in his, crossing them on her breast.

Isla Who?

Mackenzie Take thee, Isla.

Isla Not Howard.

Mackenzie Sh. Sh. Sh. Sh.

Isla Is your name Howard?

Mackenzie kisses her.

Mackenzie I, Howard, take thee Isla to wife.

Isla You've no got English blood?

Mackenzie I vow to love you.

Isla I couldnie love an Englishman.

Mackenzie Quiet.

Isla What?

Mackenzie I vow to honour you. I vow to cleave to you. By my word. By my honour. By my truth. As a plain sinner and a man.

Isla Are you asking me to marry you?

Mackenzie Do you need more than that?

Isla What do you mean?

Mackenzie We're man and wife.

Isla No.

Mackenzie In God's eyes. In my eyes. In your eyes. This is our moment.

Isla I still feel sick.

Mackenzie Isla.

A Woman stands at an open window.

Isla I need more than this.

Mackenzie Nemesis.

Isla In the eyes of the law. In the eyes of the world.

Mackenzie Catching up on me.

Isla God's in a church.

Mackenzie He's up there, just beyond the blackout Isla. I know. He's watching me.

Isla Mrs Paterson down our road.

Mackenzie Will you marry me?

Isla The two old ladies.

Mackenzie Will you marry me?

Isla Aye I will. I will so.

Mackenzie Oh God.

Isla I'll do that.

She stands in front of him. He takes her hand. Kisses it gently.

Mackenzie Oh my God.

A Woman further up the road lights a cigarette.

Maggie

Hills of the North rejoice,
Valley and lowland sing.

Maggie is singing and frying bacon.

Hark to the advent voice,
La-la-la-la-la-la,
Though absent long my Lord is nigh,
He judgement brings and . . .

The smell of that. Isla. Does that not make your mouth
water? Does that not make your heart sing. Isla. I'm
salivating myself. I've a good fire built up here. Isla. Come
on lassie. You'll not want the bacon to burn. Isla. Don't
tell me you're not hungry. I know you're hungry. A bit
fried bread. That'll do you nice.

1943
Alec's coming down the road.

Alec Is that you? Isla? Is it you? Is it? For shame Isla.
Where are you? Come on hen. My hen. What is it? Eh?
Eh? Isla. Is it some man? Is it? Eh? Is it some man at you?
Eh? Remember you're my daughter. Isla. Man. Come here.
Man. Come on out here. Get your filthy stinking hands off
her. Come on. Come on. I know men. Do I not? Come on
now. Eh? Eh? What do you think I'm gonnie do. Do you
think I'm gonnie eat you? Is that what you think? Is it?
Eh? Eh? I'm no gonnie eat you. I'm no. I'm no gonnie eat
you. Eh? Man. Eh? Eh? Eat you? I'm gonnie get my hands
round your damn throat an' I'm gonnie squeeze the life
out of you. I am. I am so. Squeeze the damn . . .

Isla You'll wake the whole street.

Alec Who the hell's that?

Isla Who do you think it is?

Alec Is that you?

Isla Father.

Alec Isla.

Isla You're drunk.

Alec I am that.

Isla Come on.

Alec You've no been playing the whore have you?

Mackenzie Do you want a hand?

Alec Who's he?

Isla Mackenzie.

Alec Who the hell is he?

Mackenzie I want to marry your daughter.

Alec A damn sailor.

Isla Come on in.

Alec No a damn sailor. You're no marryin' a sailor.

Isla He's a good man.

Alec Is he so. He will be one of the few then.

Isla So he is.

Alec Are you?

Mackenzie What?

Alec Simple enough question son. Are you a good man?

Mackenzie We all have our faults.

Alec Is that right? And what might yours be.

Isla Father.

Alec Here's a man wants to marry my daughter. I've a right . . .

Isla Stop it.

Alec Aye. Well you've a good face. I'll give you that. A sailor wi' a good face. First time for everything. You'll get plenty rum then. Eh? Eh? A good sailor. Well. I'll be damned.

1944
Maggie

> Hark to the advent voice,
> Valley and lowland sing,
> Though absent long your Lord is nigh,
> He judgement brings and fealty.

Isla's at the door.

I mind when I was in your condition. The hunger. See me when I had you in my belly. Down on my hunkers by this very fireplace. Great big belly I had. Eating coal out the scuttle. An' I'm thinking, 'I don't want to eat this.' But I'm eating it all the same. Ramming it into my mouth I am, so I've got coal dust all down my chin. An' your father comes in an' he thinks they'll be coming to cart me off. 'What do you think you're doing?' he says. An' I smile at him an' I know my teeth are all black. 'What are you, are you blind?' say I. 'I'm eating coal.' An' I'm down there on my hunkers an' I get on my dignity wi' the coal dust all down my chin. 'I'm doing what my body tells me,' say I and I bite into a beeswax candle. One of the tall ones. No that I want to. I don't want to. I want the coal. But I'm showin' him, so I'm munchin' on this candle. 'Guy funny body you've got,' he says. 'It's done you fine well enough,' say I. An' that shuts his mouth.

Isla sits at the table.

There's my girl. My lovely girl. Your father. Oh he was a proud man. He was a good-looking man. Before he got his belly on him.

Maggie puts the food in front of Isla.

Him an' me on a Friday night. Up the town. Him in his suit. Me in my beads. Parading. That's what we were doing. (*Beat.*) I've more I can make to you. (*Beat.*) We turned many a head. Your father an' me. In wur young days. (*Beat.*) You've got to see to yourself. Take care of yourself. You an' yon wee precious life that's growin' inside you. Don't think I don't know. I know. I know. (*Beat.*) You have your baby. You get it out. Get it done. Then you can start over. Start over. Start over again.

1943
Mackenzie's on his own. The Woman walks up the road. She sees Mackenzie. Stops. Watches him from a distance. Smokes.

Mackenzie Every woman I see. Every woman that passes me. I'm looking under their hats. I'm checking them out. Is it you? Is it? Cath. My love. Smile Cath the world's watchin'. A pair of legs wi' a crooked seam. A clicking pair of heels. Straighten up that seam Cath. I come out in a cold sweat. I need you to take care of me Isla. I'm skulking past policemen. I'm pulling up the collar of my raincoat. I'm going through with this marriage. Do you hear me?

The Woman licks her fingers and straightens up the seam on her stocking.

The skies might fall. You'd still have stocking to your legs.
Cath. I know. Don't think I don't know. I'm going through
with my marriage an' you'll not stop me. I could be dead
next week. Scarlet mouth puckered to take a cigarette.
You've a cruel mouth Cath. See these hands. See them.
Look at the shake on these hands. Shield me Isla. Help me.
My Cath has a pair of pelvis bones sticking out that could
cut you in two. I'm going ahead with this. Be my wife, Isla.
My woman, Isla. My good wife. Love me cherish me. As I
love and cherish . . . Keep me safe from harm. One day at
a time. One day. Step by step.

The Woman blows out smoke.

Step by step by step.

She puts the cigarette out.

Cath.

The Woman turns. Blackout.

SCENE 4

1944
Isla sitting at the table, eating. Maggie watching her. It's
breakfast time. There's a ring of the postman's bicycle bell.

Maggie My God. Did you hear that?

Isla What?

Maggie Your Faither's late for his breakfast.

Isla What's wrong.

Maggie Go an' get the post for me.

Isla What for?

Maggie Run away will you. Go on. Go on.

Isla Maggie . . .

Maggie Don't you call me that.

The postman's bicycle bell rings.

Go on. Go on. It's no much I ask you to do.

Isla I'm having my breakfast.

Maggie I'll keep it hot.

Isla What's wrong wi' you?

Maggie You'll go an' get the post off the postman an' if your Faither catches you comin' back you'll tell him you went down to Sadie's for the bread.

Isla I haven't got any bread.

Maggie You'll tell him Sadie was out of bread. You'll not show him the post. You'll bring the post to me.

Isla sits back with her arms folded.

Hurry up.

Silence.

Oh my God. Isla. Help me. I'm askin' you.

Silence.

I've bills in the post Isla. I'm askin' for your help. I canny let your Faither see the bills. He's no got the money to pay them. An' neither have I.

Silence.

That was a fine big wedding we gave you.

Noises from upstairs.

No that I'm feart of your Faither. Help me Isla. It's no for mysel' I've spent the money.

Isla You'll have to pay some time.

Maggie You look at me. Do I look like . . . I've no even got a decent hat to go the messages in.

Isla He'll have to know some time.

Maggie Did you no hear the ding of that bell.

Isla Maggie . . .

Maggie It's only the once your Faither's hit me. For by I spat in his face. I canny mind what I spat in his face for. But I mind him hittin' me. He's comin'. Help me.

Isla My Faither never hit you.

Maggie Aye he did.

Isla My Faither never lifted a hand to you.

Maggie You've always loved him the best. Don't you think I don't know that. It's easy for a man to be loved.

Noise from the bedroom.

He's comin', Isla.

Isla gets up.

You put those bills in your pocket. You keep your hand on them.

Isla leaves.

You keep them deep in your pocket. That's my hen. You're your Mother's own wee hen. Mind now. Sadie's. Sadie's for the bread.

1943
There's a Woman out taking the air far off in the darkness, standing, leaning, at her ease.

Isla and Mackenzie are in the torchlight. At the back kitchen door. In the late night.

Isla We'll love each other, won't we. Always. Always.

Mackenzie We'll see.

Isla Come on Mackenzie. Let's be romantic.

Mackenzie Right you are then.

Isla You look daft.

Mackenzie I'm no a romantic sort of a person.

Isla Aye you are.

Mackenzie Aye I'm not.

Isla You are. You are so.

Mackenzie I am not.

Isla I know you.

   Silence.

I do. Don't I. There's no other body in this whole wide world that knows you like I do. Is there? Is there?

Mackenzie What do you know?

Isla Underneath it all. You're really quite nice.

Mackenzie Am I?

Isla We'll always tell each other everything won't we.

Mackenzie What's this always you keep flinging at me. You're my woman. I'll tell you what I think it's good for you to know.

Isla We'll be honest.

Mackenzie Step by step.

Isla Give me a kiss.

Mackenzie You're daft you are.

Isla Are you not gonnie kiss me.

Mackenzie You should marry some fine young chap wi' a cushy number an' prospects.

Isla I don't like fine young chaps.

Mackenzie Marry a right bastard an' you get what's comin' to you.

Isla I don't like that word.

Mackenzie I'm sorry.

Isla I'll not have bad language.

Mackenzie Isla . . .

Isla Mackenzie . . .

Mackenzie I could be dead next week.

Isla Cross your fingers an' pray to God when you say that.

Mackenzie I'm praying alright.

Isla Do you really want me?

Mackenzie Aye. I do.

Isla Well then.

Mackenzie What?

Isla That's alright, then.

Mackenzie Aye.

Isla As long as you want me.

Mackenzie Aye. I do that. I want you alright.

*The torches go out and the Woman in the far distance
shivers in the cold, turns up the collar of her coat and
goes home.*

1944
*Isla slams the bills down on to the table. Maggie looks at
them. Each one of them. Then she stuffs them down into
the pocket of her apron.*

Maggie See you've got to keep things from them. You've
got to keep your own counsel. Never give yoursel' away.
Keep a bit of yoursel' private.

Isla What'll you do with them.

Maggie I'll handle your Faither in my own time. I'll see to
him.

Blackout.

SCENE 5

1943
*The wedding day. Alec is filling a hip flask from a bottle of
rum. He's half-dressed in morning dress, in his shirt sleeves
and his waistcoat. Whistling and singing.*

Alec

Oh I will take you home Cathleen,
Across the Ocean wild and wide,
To where your heart has ever been,
Since first your were my bonnie bride.

*He pockets the hip flask. Stands at the mirror over the
fire tying his tie. A dove-grey cravat. Pins it with a
golden pin.*

The roses all have left your cheeks,

I've watched them fade away and die.
Your voice is sad when e'er you speak,
And tears bedim your loving eye.
Oh I will take you back Cathleen,
To where your heart will feel no pain,
And when the fields are fresh and green,
I will take you to your home again.

Isla, in her wedding dress, stands at the door. Alec sees her in the mirror. Turns to look.

Aye.

Isla Is that all you've got to say.

Alec My bonnie lass. My bonnie wee lassie. Here. (*He gets out the hip flask.*) I'll give you a toast in good Navy Rum. You'll not ask me where I got it. May you be as happy through the years as your Mother and I have been. (*He drinks.*) If you can do that you'll be doing well. Here. (*He hands her the flask.*) That'll set you up.

Isla Pa Pa.

Alec My bonnie lass.

Isla I wanted to say . . .

Alec Drink.

She shrugs and swallows.

You could always take a drink well. If I've taught you nothing else I've taught you that. My own wee girl. My own. My ain one. You were always your Pa Pa's best girl. My dark princess. My wee girl sitting at ma knee . . . (*He sits down.*) Come on. Come here.

She sits on his knee.

Cheeky wee thing you were. You in your red dresses. Your mother always had you done up fine. Your wee red boots.

I like to see a woman dressed. I'm that proud of you. You've been a good girl. A good, good girl. Don't you tell me you haven't had the opportunity to be otherwise. I know. I know men. Don't I just. We've got wur faults. We're good creatures at the bottom but faults, we've got faults. I know what I'm talkin' about. Your Mother an' me we could always trust you. We've always been proud of you. You've kept your goodness. That's a fine thing. It's a pure gift you've got to give to your Mackenzie an' I know he appreciates it. He's a rare good man. A gift, that's what it is you're bringing to him. The greatest gift a woman can give to a man. An' he'll know. You'll belong to him. Only to him. You listen to your Faither. I'm proud of you. You're giving him your goodness. (*He takes hold of her chin and strokes her cheek.*) Not that I'm drunk. I'm no drunk.

Isla I know.

Alec You'll no find me drunk this day. If I drink your health now an' again that's all I'll do.

Isla I don't . . .

Alec A man has his disappointments Isla.

Isla I know you . . .

Alec A man can drink his own daughter's health on her wedding day.

Isla You do what . . .

Alec Can he not? Eh? Can he not?

Isla We'll drink the one to the other. (*She gets off his knee. Toasts him with the hip flask.*) Here's tae you.

Alec Mind your Mother now. That was a different tale. My Maggie. My wicked Maggie. No virgin bride in all her innocence my Maggie. Walked up the aisle carrying her hummock in front of her, carrying it for all to see. Dressed in white an' smilin' to either side. Daring them, any one of them to say a word to her. Daring God hissel'. My Maggie. My wicked Maggie. She'll go to Hell my Maggie. God'll never smile on her as he's smilin' on you this day. Did she no lay wi' me on the Isle of Millport. She cam' away on her holidays wi' me. Seventeen years old. Defyin' them all. I took your Mother on a train. You take my meanin'. I took her. Scrappy affair it was. Us both wi' wur clothes still on. Down the corridor, between the carriages, on a train to Millport. You've your gift to your husband. You've the gift to your own sweet self, on your wedding night. My wicked Maggie. See I never knew. If I . . .

Maggie behatted at the door.

Maggie You're the one and only love of my life. That's what you are.

Alec Am I so? Am I that so?

Maggie Have I not made you my whole life.

Alec Tell me Maggie. Tell me.

Maggie Your back collar stud's undone.

Alec I don't know.

Maggie Come here an' I'll see to it.

Alec I don't know.

Maggie Have I not brought up your children to be whole and good.

Alec You were that headstrong Maggie.

Maggie I've brought them up right.

Alec Was it me?

Maggie Does it matter now?

Alec For if you did it with me like that. There on that train wi' the draught blowin' roun' wur bare parts . . .

Maggie I've been your wife these twenty-seven years.

Alec Could you not have gone wi' any other man.

Maggie It was war time.

Alec War time then.

Maggie Strange things happen in a war.

Alec War time now.

Maggie So many never came back.

Alec Was there more than me? You're aye a good-lookin' woman Maggie. You're my torture Maggie.

Maggie I've always loved you.

Alec Always.

Maggie Did I not pay enough for that dress to be made right. You get away from yon fire. You'll have it burnt before the day's right started.

Alec My wee girl.

Maggie She's not your wee girl.

Alec I've an hour or two yet.

Maggie She's a woman grown. Let me look at you.

Isla I wanted to say thank you to you both.

Alec What have you got to thank us for?

Maggie Turn round.

Alec You've nothing to thank us for. The greatest gift God gives on to the earth is a child to love. You've been a child both lovely and loving.

Maggie You're beautiful so that's alright.

Alec Blessed little children. Blessed, blessed children. I've watched you grow. You've made me proud.

Maggie This is your day.

Alec Bless you.

Maggie We've done wur best for you.

Alec Bless you.

Maggie See an' enjoy your day.

Alec Seeing you in that.

Maggie It needed taking in . . .

Alec I mind your Mother in that.

Maggie A wee bit taken in . . .

Alec Seventeen year old.

Dance-band music from the wedding reception.
Maggie's voice singing 'My love is like a red, red rose'.
Mackenzie's on his own. Leaning. Taking the air.

Maggie

Till a' the seas gang dry my dear
An' rocks melt in the sun
Oh I will love thee still my dear
While the sands of life shall run.

A **Woman** *walks down the street.*

Mackenzie Cath. Cath. Cath. (*He's speaking to the Woman as she walks.*) My dead brother. Cath. What that did to me. Eh? What did that no do to me? Cath. I'll not say we didn't have good moments. Cath. Look at me. Photos of me. They'll be doing this day. Do I not look fine? Spruced up and immaculate. Spit an' polish. She's a good girl. Cath let me be. My brother. I thought we were charmed the pair of us. Cath. We're none of us charmed. Cath. Stay away from me. Cath. Cath.

The Woman stops as she gets to him.

Woman Are you talking to me?

Mackenzie Cath.

Woman I'm afraid you must be mistaken.

Mackenzie I beg your pardon.

Woman Please . . .

Mackenzie I'm sorry I . . .

Woman Could I have a light?

Mackenzie Of course . . .

Woman Look at your hands.

Mackenzie What?

Woman Are you cold?

Mackenzie No.

Woman You're shaking.

Mackenzie I've been married this day.

Woman That's enough to make a body shake.

Mackenzie My wedding day.

Woman Congratulations. Thank you. (*She holds out the lighter.*)

Mackenzie What?

Woman Cath eh? (*She's reading the name on the lighter.*) Is that your wife. (*She gives it him back.*)

Mackenzie You need more than a good moment or two.

Woman That's right.

Mackenzie In a life.

Woman Why not.

Mackenzie That's right.

Woman Good luck to you. (*She walks off.*)

Mackenzie Cath.

Woman No. Not me.

Mackenzie You have to grab at life. That's what I say. Grab and hold hard.

Woman That's right. That's very right.

Mackenzie Cath. Damn you Cath. It's my wedding day. Here.

The Woman's walking away.

Woman Not me son. Not me.

Mackenzie Do you want this? (*The lighter.*)

Woman Eh?

Mackenzie You take this.

Woman Why?

Mackenzie I've had my use out of it.

Woman I can't . . .

Mackenzie I want you to have it.

Woman Why not?

Mackenzie For luck.

Woman After all.

She takes the lighter. Isla's in the doorway.

Good fortune.

Isla They're wondering where you are.

Mackenzie Aye.

Isla Who were you talking to?

Mackenzie Some woman.

Isla Come an' dance.

Mackenzie In a minute.

Isla Are you sorry?

Mackenzie What?

Isla You're not sorry?

Mackenzie Here.

Isla Why?

Mackenzie Come here.

Isla You come here.

Mackenzie Where did you get to be so . . .

Isla What?

Mackenzie Insolent Madam. That's you. Cheeky wee besom. That's you.

Isla Who was she?

Mackenzie I'm going to catch you.

Isla Why were you talking to her?

Mackenzie I'll get you.

Isla Mackenzie.

Mackenzie Run. (*He catches her. Tickles her.*)

Isla No.

Mackenzie I've got you. I've got you.

Isla I'm your wife.

He stops.

Mackenzie Isla. (*He's holding her.*)

Isla What is it? (*Beat.*) Mac. What?

Mackenzie I've a present for you.

Isla I like presents.

He reaches into his inside pocket. Gives her a small black leather bible.

That's a very serious present. (*She opens it.*) Forever and always. That's a long time. What a long, long time.

The Woman with the cigarette lighter lights a cigarette in the far, far distance.
The dance band in the hall playing 'Red Sails in the Sunset'.
Maggie's in the doorway, drinking and singing.
Isla and Mackenzie dance. Round and round and round. The circle of their dance widens. When they reach the Woman, the dance stops. Mackenzie takes the Woman in his arms and Isla watches.

Alec Dance wi' yer old man. Come to my arms wee hen.

Maggie watches and sings on. Isla and Alec dance.

You'll do well to let him be. I see your eyes. I know what you're thinking. It's a wise woman that knows when to keep her mouth shut. For a man to marry is a great thing. He's giving up everything. A woman now that's a fair different story. A woman, she gains everything. Position. A place in the eyes of the world. On her finger for all to see she bears the mark of being wanted, the mark of her belonging. A ring. It's what she's been brought up for. The summit of her ambition. The goal of all her training. Look. See him dancing there. Do they not look well together? Aye, she can dance. She can dance alright. Look how they move the both of them. What if he strays. What if? You let him be. You smile an' he'll come runnin' back. Mind me what I'm sayin' now. Mind. These words are the gleanings of the years. I've learnt. I'm wise. Oh yes I'm the wise one. Mind me. Mind what I'm sayin'. He's a fine big man. An' you've caught him. That's a great thing. Now you break him in gently. Be canny. Never nag. Give him that much freedom he never knows he's been caught. Keep his meals hot an' his bed well aired. Keep yersel' pure for him. An' mind you wear some perfume of an evening. Mind that. There's nothing like the smell of a woman's perfume. Mind all that an' he'll come home to you and he'll bear with him armfuls of flowers an' a heart full of gratitude that he'll lay at your feet. Gratitude'll hold a man longer than any youthful idea of love. Gratitude's what makes a bond. And guilt. I know. Do I not know. Love now. Love. That merely makes the marriage. You smile my wee girl. Smile. Smile. Let your beauty shine forth on this glorious day. For you've made your old Father a happy, happy man.

Blackout.

Act Two

SCENE I

The light is on Mackenzie in the darkness. He's wearing a navy-blue greatcoat.

Mackenzie I'm on the deck. I've ropes all round me. Lyin' there. Ropes as thick as a wrist. Ropes thick as a man's thigh. All round me. It's cold. Cold. Cold. I'm lookin' up. The sky's flat grey an' the sea's all empty. I'm alone. I've no gloves an' my hands are chapped. Where's my God damn gloves. Some bugger's pinched them. My hands are chapped wi' the cold. I've had boils in my beard an' the doctor's said my blood's bad. I'm a sinner. What does he expect? An evil man. Eh? Eh? The sea's empty an' the sky's empty. And I thank you God. Me standin' there in amongst the ropes on yon cold deck. I thank you God for the empty sky. I can see hope in an empty sky.

Maggie

> I to the hills will lift mine eyes,
> From whence doth come mine aid.
> My safety cometh from the Lord,
> Who heaven and earth hath made.

Mackenzie I've the phones on. I'm listening. There's nothing. I'm that quiet. I'm that still. God you know I'm a Heathen deep down at the bottom of me. But I'm a good Heathen. You know that. I've the phones on my ears. All is silence. Thank you God. There's no bloody subs this side. Thank you, God. Boom. You've filled the world for me. Boom. Boom. You've exploded a bloody torpedo in my ear drums. Come on play the white man. Where was the bloody sub God. Come on. Come on. Boom. And my

138

world's all red. Boom. Easy come, easy go. Eh God.

Maggie Bring my boys back. Bring my boys safe back to me.

1943
The sun's shining. Isla and Mackenzie are sitting on the raincoat, looking out over the Firth of Clyde.

Mackenzie You canny call these boats.

Isla I'll call them what I like.

Mackenzie There's no dignity in a boat.

Isla They're floating aren't they.

Mackenzie Big bloody things like that lying at their rest in all their majesty. These are ships, woman, ships.

Isla You'll not get me on one.

Mackenzie Scotland's glory these are.

The Woman is in the distance.

Isla Who's that?

Mackenzie Welded, riveted, fitted. Right here. Right here.

Isla She's lookin' at us.

Mackenzie I like the sea. I love the sea. I'll be a sailor all my life.

Isla She knows you.

Mackenzie When this war's over an' I've seen it through I'll join the Merchant Navy an' you'll be a sailor's wife an' you'll come wi' me an' we'll visit the far-flung corners of this world. You an' me Isla. You an' me.

Isla Who is she Mac?

Mackenzie looks at the Woman. She comes towards them.

Mackenzie Just some woman that's all.

The Woman stands above them. Floats a newspaper cutting down into Mackenzie's lap. Isla picks it up.

Isla That's us. That's our wedding photo. Do I know you?

Cath Your landlady told me where to come.

Isla The old one?

Cath Aye.

Isla Peggy that'll be. I don't know you.

Mackenzie yanks Isla to her feet. Pulls at her to get her away.

What is it? What is it?

He starts to turn, holding on to her.

Your raincoat, Mackenzie. (*She breaks free of him. Runs back. Picks up the raincoat. Runs back to Mackenzie.*) My God, Mackenzie. What is it?

He grabs her hand.

Mackenzie Come wi' me. Come wi' me. (*He starts to run.*)

Isla You're hurting me.

He's pulling her along with him.

Mackenzie Isla.

Isla You're hurting my hand.

He runs with her. She stumbles and falls. He catches her, holds her in his arms.

Mackenzie Guitars. You an' me. Eh Wilf? Singin' for wur supper. Tiger Bay. What the Hell we were doing there. Brat you were. Right there. Right there beside me. I'll take care of you wee lad. I'll see you alright. Has my sin been so great Lord. My good Lord. Take a look around you. Take a good, good look. You tell me why you're cursing me. Eh Lord? My wee brother in the sea clinging to his life. My wee brother. He liked the girls. My great good Lord up there in your fine Heaven. What was the harm my wee brother did unto you that you should kill him there in that cold sea. (*He jerks Isla to her feet.*) Get up. She's behind us yet. Come on. (*He drags her behind him, running still.*)

Isla I can't run any more.

Mackenzie Come on.

Isla I've no got the shoes for it.

Mackenzie Take your damn shoes off.

Isla I can't run in my bare feet.

Mackenzie shakes her.

Mackenzie Run will you. Run will you. Run. Run.

Isla She knows where we're staying.

Mackenzie We're no goin' back there. (*Beat.*) Come on. Come on. (*Beat.*) Don't greet. Dinny greet.

Isla You're hurting me.

Mackenzie Move will you woman.

Isla Who is she? (*Beat.*) We canny keep just running.

Mackenzie There Isla. There. There, there, there. (*He wipes her face with his hands.*) No time for that now.

They run on.

Isla What is it? What is it?

Mackenzie Come on.

Isla Who is she?

Mackenzie stops.

Who is she?

Mackenzie She's my wife.

Isla Don't be daft.

Silence.

Oh my God.

Mackenzie sits down.

I'm expectin'.

Mackenzie Are you.

Isla It's early days yet. I've a baby in me.

Mackenzie I'm sorry.

Isla All that runnin'. (*Beat.*) What's her name?

Mackenzie Cath.

Isla An' she's your wife.

Mackenzie Aye.

Isla Have we stopped? Is that it? Have we stopped running now? She's your wife?

Silence.

What does that make me? And the wain that's inside me. What am I?

1944
In the back room. Alec stands over the table. Maggie is sitting there. Alec holds his hand out. Maggie looks at him.

*Alec bangs the table with the flat of his hand. Maggie digs
her hand into her apron pocket. She brings out the bills.
She hands them to Alec. He looks at them. He hits her.
About the shoulders. She takes it.*

Alec You've shamed me.

   *He leaves the room. Maggie leans on the table with her
   head on her arms.*

1943
*On the hill above the Firth of Clyde, in the sunshine,
Mackenzie, Cath and Isla are sitting side by side by side.*

Isla It's a beautiful view. You really can't beat the view.
There's no other country can beat Scotland. I've always
said that. If we had the weather. If we just had the weather.

Cath I've two kids. Tam's six and Jackie's three.

Isla It's a pity about the weather.

Cath Jackie's my love. She's like her father. A right wee
charmer. She's his eyes.

Isla He's a handsome man.

Cath And curls she's got.

Isla Has she?

Cath Of course she's dark.

Isla And you've children.

Mackenzie They're no my kids.

Cath Don't you start that. Tam's quite the wee man. Six
years old an' he's got his boats all lined up an' he can tell
you the frigates an' he can tell you the destroyers.

Isla Ships aren't they?

Cath A right wee man. Cock of the walk he is. Like his father before him.

Silence.

It wasnie clever to put the picture in the paper.

Mackenzie D'you think I did that?

Isla My Father was that proud.

Cath What did you think was gonnie happen?

Mackenzie I hate you. May God forgive me.

Cath He might. I'll not. I'm gonnie get you Mackenzie. If I have tae go so far as to have you put in the gaol then that's what I'll do. I'm gonnie get you for what you've done to me. I'm sorry for your woman don't you think I'm not. But I'm no gonnie think about her. I'm gonnie think about mysel' an' my wains an' I'll get you.

Isla Would you excuse me. I have to be going now.

Mackenzie Stay where you are.

Isla Oh no please Mackenzie you must see I . . .

Mackenzie You're no the one should leave.

Isla Let me go.

Blackout.

SCENE 2

1943
Maggie's sitting at the table. The light from the hall's shining into the room. Isla's standing at the sink in her slip. She's washing and washing and washing her body with a cloth. Washing on top of the slip.

Maggie A woman has to cleave to a man. That's what I say. A woman has her man. A woman needs her man. I'm with your Faither. I'm with him yet. Don't you think we've not had wur troubles. A wee quarrel. You'll have plenty of those through the years. At least let me put the light on. You're a married lady, you're not some wee girl. The ring you've got on your finger. That's a blessed thing that ring. You'll no sin against that ring. (*Beat.*) Ma wee hen. Will I no put the light on? Isla. You'll spoil your nice . . . your Father could come down here. Isla. Let me put on the light. (*Beat.*) What is this? What is it? I'll have no trouble in my family. Not in my family. If we had on the light. I don't want you down with a cold.

Alec's at the door.

Alec What's the noise?

Maggie Cover yourself.

Alec This time of night.

Maggie D'you hear me?

Alec A man's his work in the morn.

Maggie Get yourself covered.

Isla Look at me.

Maggie What is it? What is it?

Isla Look at me.

Maggie I've my nice dressing gown here.

Alec It'll be her condition. That'll be what it is. Maggie.

Maggie I'll not have this trouble in my house.

Alec You wi' your first wain. You were maudlin.

Isla Look at me. Look at me.

Maggie We're lookin'. We're all lookin'. An' a right eyeful that's what we're gettin'. Where's your modesty. Is your Faither no a man right enough that you should strip yoursel' under his eye. Alec you'll get away to your bed.

Alec A wee cup of tea. That's what she wants. Plenty of sugar. She keeps a good house your Mother.

Maggie You've yer work.

Isla Look. Look at me. Look at me.

Alec A wee dram.

Maggie I'll deal wi' it.

Alec She'll catch cold.

Maggie Get to bed.

Alec Wettin' all her parts like that.

Maggie Go on. Get. Get.

Alec goes. Maggie picks up the dressing gown and puts it round Isla.

Letting your father see you like that. Your body. Your breasts sticking out through. Giving him his eyeful right enough.

Isla Look at me. Look at me. Look at me.

Maggie slaps her. Isla stops.

Maggie Have you no shame. Sit down. Sit down.

Isla sits at the table.

There's no excuse for this. None whatsoever. You're a grown woman.

Isla I'll not go back.

Maggie Giving your father a red face.

Isla I can't go back.

Maggie Don't talk nonsense.

Isla I'm soiled by him.

Maggie A good night's sleep.

Isla He's made me dirty.

Maggie Sleep's what you need. Sleep's all you need.

There's a knocking at the back door. Silence.

There you are.

Isla No.

Maggie For goodness sake.

Isla It's him.

Maggie This time of night.

Isla Don't let him in.

Maggie Don't talk daft.

Isla Please Mother.

Maggie Thank the good Lord you've a man that'll bother tae come chasin' away after you.

Isla Mother.

Maggie There's many a many wouldnie bother their heads.

Isla I can't talk to him.

Maggie There's a handkerchief in the pocket of my dressing gown. Dry your eyes. Here.

Isla I'm that ashamed.

Maggie reaches into the pocket.

Maggie Here. That's it. Never let a man think he's got the better of you. Blow. A good blow. That's my girl. Now. (*She opens the door.*) Aye. Come away in. Come you away in. I don't know what's between you. I don't want to know. I mind my own business. Sit down.

Mackenzie sits at the table.

Now you. The both of you. You make your peace between you. For your own two sakes. For the wain's sake. I want no trouble in my house. (*She stops at the door.*) Mind an' keep yer noise down. I've my man asleep up the stairs.

Silence.

Right you are then. (*She goes.*)

Isla My Father's got his work tomorrow.

Mackenzie Of course.

Isla She worries about him.

Mackenzie Aye.

Isla He drinks.

Mackenzie I know.

Isla Mind he's a nice drinker. There's no harm in him. Poor wee man. No harm at all. I'm gonnie break his heart. If I'd lain wi' you on that raincoat. We'd not be in this mess, would we? Would we?

Mackenzie I don't know.

Isla Virtue is it's own reward. Is that not what they say? She thinks he's all she's got left.

Mackenzie Does she?

Isla Mind she's wrong about that.

Mackenzie Is she?

Isla She's got me hasn't she.

Pause.

Hasn't she?

Mackenzie I suppose . . .

Isla Me an' the wain.

Mackenzie Isla . . .

Isla Inside my belly.

Mackenzie I love you.

Isla Don't.

Mackenzie It's the truth.

Isla A brat I've got in me. Your brat.

Mackenzie Please . . .

Isla Your bastard. (*She spins the ring on the table.*) I've got my Mother.

They both watch the ring spinning.

You could have taken me on your damn raincoat. I'd have succumbed eventually. Don't we all. Don't we all lie flat on our backs and part our legs for you. (*She catches the ring.*) Will she divorce you. Mackenzie. Will she?

Mackenzie She's a Pape.

Isla I see.

Mackenzie I was a boy when I married her.

Isla Is that right?

Mackenzie I made a mistake.

Isla Oh well.

Mackenzie I love you.

Isla Uncle Keir kissed that ring. Uncle Gordie blessed it. Auntie Ann wet it with her tears.

Mackenzie It's dark.

Isla I like the dark.

Mackenzie I'm scared of the dark.

Isla And you a big man.

Mackenzie Let me put the light on.

Isla Never show a man yer whole body bare. My Mother told me that. Keep your secrets. Never show a man all yer body.

Mackenzie As long as I pay her we'll can live together. She'll not tell.

Isla You've children. Mackenzie. Oh God. Oh God.

Mackenzie There's not a soul'll know outside the three of us.

Isla God'll know.

Mackenzie There'll be no difference to us. You'll have a ring to your finger.

Isla I'll have that.

Mackenzie I'll never leave you.

Isla Will you no.

Mackenzie We'll be alright then. The two of us. You an' me.

Isla God looks down.

Mackenzie We'll can go on as we are.

Isla I don't want the light on. I don't want the light on at all.

Cath outside by the window lights the lighter, lights a cigarette.

Mackenzie If we were not meant to take our pleasure, the women and the men. What for did You give us the tools to take our pleasure with.

Mackenzie takes a light from the lighter. Lets it burn. Takes Cath in his arms.

Jesus bids us shine with a pure clear light,
Like a little candle burning in the night,
The world is filled with darkness,
We can make it shine,
You in your small corner,
And I in mine.

Snaps the lighter out. Holds Cath tight.

We're in the water Cath. Him an' me. Wilf. (*Beat.*) It's dark. An' I'm yellin' 'Where are you son? Wilf.' (*Beat.*) I'm callin' him. 'Wilf!' (*Beat.*) Listen. Listen. (*Beat.*) Nothin'. (*Beat.*) My wee brother, Cath. (*Beat.*) Nothin' (*Beat.*) Listen. (*Beat.*) I'm alone in the water. They've killed my brother Cath. Does that no deserve punishment? (*Beat.*) Clear eyes he had an' a twinkle. And I was to look after him. D'you mind his drawings. Cath. Cowboys wi' cigarettes hangin' out the corner of their mouths an' wee dogs peein' up against lampposts. What I've done to you. It's very small beer indeed.

She lifts her head from his shoulder. Looks at him.

Will you let me be.

She moves out of his arms. Silence. He catches her hand. Holds it hard.

Will you put me in the gaol? Will you do that?

Silence.

Aye. Alright Cath. Alright.

Blackout.

SCENE 3

Mackenzie Hey you. You. Did You take a wee nap was that it? Poor old Fella. An awful lot's expected of you. Keeping up the natural order. What were you doing? Did you take a wee break. Were you watchin' them dancin', the Daughters of Men? Right nice wee things. Eh? And all your own work. Guitars an' they waggle their hips. Look there. Look there. The wee one wi' the lips an' the ukulele. Can she no sing. Take care of her. Keep her safe from harm. A wee toy to grace your universe. We're all of us toys. Eh? Is that not right?

1944
Maggie and Isla are in the back living room.

Isla My lamb. Kicking at my ribs. My lamb. Making me take notice. Turning over inside of me. Making me go on. It an' me. You'll not take my child away from me. My very own. You've not got the right to take my child from me.

Maggie You've got to make a new life for yourself.

Isla My life's here in me.

Maggie You'll find another man.

Isla We belong together, it an' me.

Maggie You were bonnie before.

Isla I don't want another man.

Maggie You're bonnie yet. You need a man. Too bonnie for your own good. You'll want one. You'll want one alright.

Isla Don't tell me.

Maggie You'll not get one wi' a wain hangin' at yer breast.

Isla I know what I want.

Maggie An' me. Eh? What about me? Eh? What about what I want. Eh? Answer me that. Do I no get a look in? What do I want? Playin' the fine heroine. You wi' yer face straight an' never a smile about yer mouth these dark days. What about me? We could all do wi' a smile. I've seen it, the scorn in your eyes. I've seen it. Don't you think I haven't. You an' yer Faither. I can't go into a shop now . . . He's . . . Your Father . . . He's taken my pride from me. An' you're askin' me. Askin' me. Tendin' to a wain. Years at a wain's beck an' call. I've my own big son in prison camp in Germany. I'm tired. I'm very, very tired, I get by. Day by day by day, I get by. I've your brother on the submarines. My mind's full up. There's not the room inside my head to take on another thing. Isla. Are you listening to me? Isla. I pray. I'm walking round here. I'm cooking, I'm no here. I'm cleaning. I'm all the time talking to God. I'm keeping my sons alive. I'm that long on my knees at the side of my bed in the night. I'm talking to God. I'm talking and talking. I've no room in me for a baby. We make our own way. I've no time. Each one of us, our own way. I've no room in my heart. Make your own way. I'll not tend it for you. I'll not care for it. Make your own way. I'll not look after it. Make your own way. I've had five wains of my own. I'll not start over. I can't.

Isla It'll not go on for ever, the war.

Maggie I'm that tired.

Isla You'll take care . . .

Maggie You're no listenin' to me.

Isla You'll take care of my baby for me.

Maggie There'll be war an' more war. And I'll tell you why. Men. That's why. Men are sinners and God's in his wrath.

Isla I'll go out to work.

Maggie If I could just sleep.

Isla I'll not take money from you. I'll pay for my keep. Take care of my baby for me.

Maggie Men are sinners and the good God is sick at the stench of them. I'll get the tea.

Isla Blood of your blood.

Maggie I've a nice bit of sliced sausage. Och listen hen. There'll be other babies. Aye you're lookin' at me. It's the truth I'm tellin' you an' one day you'll thank me for it. What's it gonnie be like for him eh, a wee bastard living down this road an' all they folk knowin'. There's always babies.

Isla You'll keep my baby for me.

Maggie It's a boy you're carryin' there. I know from the way it hangs. It's a boy you're bringin' into the world.

Alec comes in from work.

Alec See here what I've brought. See here what I've got for my wee girl. My own wee girl. (*He puts a Scottie dog ornament on the table.*) What some people throw out for junk. That's no junk. That was in the old man's shop round the corner from the works. Sittin' there all forlorn. We'll give that house room. We'll give that a home.

Isla Pa Pa.

Alec See its tartan collar.

Maggie Tea.

Alec It's a bitter night.

Maggie It's good an' hot.

Alec It'll want livening up.

Maggie Is that right?

Alec I'm cold to my bones.

Maggie Are you now?

Alec Look at yer dog hen. A rare wee dog. If I had a dog.

Maggie Dirty things. Dogs.

Alec That's the dog I'd have.

Isla I can type.

Alec A wee drap. A wee, wee drap.

Maggie gets the whisky.

Is there no some of that rum. Aye. A wee touch. An' a wee touch more.

Maggie It'll run out of the cup.

Alec Tip out some of the tea woman. Can ye no.

Isla I've a head for figures.

Alec A good education my family's had. They'll not hold that against me. Not any one of them. I've seen to their education.

Isla I can earn my living.

Alec What is it that you want hen?

Isla I can pay for my keep.

Alec You tell your old Pa Pa.

Isla I can work.

Alec So you can.

Isla Pa Pa.

Alec A good cup of tea.

Isla My keep an' my baby's.

Alec Warm the cockles of your heart.

Isla Please.

Alec Are you no gonnie look at your dog hen. That I brought home for you. To cheer you.

Isla Help me.

Alec Yer nice wee dog hen.

Silence.

I'm no sayin' I don't understand . . .

Maggie Men are children Isla. Take that to your heart and keep it there. In pain we bear them. God's cursed we are. And pain they give us all the long night through.

Isla No.

Alec I'm no the one that's got tae look after it.

Maggie I'm telling you.

Alec She's a good woman your Mother.

Isla I want to keep my baby.

Alec A good strong woman.

Isla 'Anything you want', that's what you said to me. 'I'll get you the moon from out of the sky if you ask me for it.' Pa Pa.

Alec I'll bide by your Mother's decision.

Isla God help me.

Alec That's it finished. I'll hear no more.

Isla You've talked about this.

Maggie We're man and wife.

Isla The two of you.

Maggie A woman cleaves to her man.

Isla And he holds to her.

Alec I've seen them lookin' at you. You walkin' down the street. You've kept yersel' nice. I'll grant you that. There's many a woman would have let hersel' go. I've seen them lookin' at you. Sorrow at their mouth an' a smile in their eyes. You send that child away. Peepin' out frae behind their curtains. I've seen them. An' you wi' yer head held high. An' your misfortune. My own proud girl. Send that child away. These folk. We live amongst these folk. Send that child where it'll have a good life. Do that for it. 'Shame,' they're sayin'. 'Shame. Shame.' An' they're shakin' their heads an' they're hidin' their smirkin' faces behind their hands. 'Shame. Shame.' I'll not have my daughter held up to this. Nor my wife. Nor any grandchild of mine. I have to walk down that street too. This is where I live. All my life I've lived here. This street knows me. It's seen my joy. It's seen my despair. I started the works in my own back yard. I'll bide by your Mother's decision. I walk down that road an' I'm naked. And don't you think they'd forget. Them behind their curtains. They've long memories. Long. Long. And your wain, he'd feel it too. You've all my love, wee girl. All my love. You give that child away. All my love. You make a good marriage for yousel'. Listen to me, what I'm sayin'. Find some rich man. Marry some big doctor. Someone that'll take you. Someone to belong to. That'll still their waggin' tongues. Marry. Marry well. Make them laugh on the other side of their damn faces.

Isla Please.

Alec Listen to yer Faither.

Isla Help me.

Maggie I'll not look after your child.

Isla Mackenzie. Mackenzie.

Alec You can't get blood out of a stone.

Isla You'll not give us house room.

Maggie No.

Isla You'll not even do that. Is this not my home.

Alec Your Mother's had enough.

Maggie You stay. Stay by all means. Stay as long as you want. An' welcome.

Isla I see.

Maggie I'm sorry hen.

Alec We're aye that.

Maggie I say my prayers for you.

Alec The both of us.

Isla Thank you.

Alec We're sorry alright.

1943

Mackenzie Heart beating? Yes. Spine intact. Legs. Yes. It's
dark. I'm cold. Why's it so God damn dark? Pulse. Yes.
My eyes. Can I see? Give us a light in your God damn
world can't you. God? Don't leave a man to grovel here.
Bowels moving. God no. Don't take my dignity. I'm
scared. God save me. Now I lay me down to sleep, I pray
the Lord my soul to keep. If I should die before I wake, I
pray the Lord my soul to take. Light God. Light. Thank
you God. God bless you sir. I can see fine well. I always
had a good pair of eyes. There's many a many has fallen
for my eyes. Eh God. I'm your boy. Oh God. Look there
God. Look there. That's my wee brother there. God. Were
you so busy? You never paid him any mind. That's my wee
brother dead over there.

1944

*Alec has a telegram in his hand. Maggie takes it from him.
He stands there. She reads the telegram. Alec sits down at
the table. Maggie puts the telegram carefully up on the
mantelshelf. She stands by Alec and cradles him in her
arms.*

Maggie

> Abide with me,
> Fast falls the eventide,
> The darkness deepens,
> Lord with me abide.
> When other help has fled,
> And comforts flee,
> Help of the helpless, oh,
> Abide with me.

Blackout.

SCENE 4

Mackenzie Terrible kind of self-pity about me now. Always was. Touch of the maudlin about me. That hacked body lyin' there. Men go from this man's navy. Men walk. Disappear. Not me. I havenie got the guts. God. You missed something out when you made me.

My cup's full and running over,
For the Lord made me,
I'm as happy as can be.

Stand up, stand up for Jesus,
Ye soldiers of the cross,
Lift high his royal banner,
It must not . . .

My cup's full and running over.

Flesh. Warm. Firm to the touch. Warm skin under my hands. I'm good wi' a woman. Grant me that. I've had plenty practice. My hands on my dead brother's body. Laid my hands on him an' the flesh gave back when I touched him. Clammy. Sick dead flesh. And I left him there. Free will. Eh God. We're all of us free agents in this best of all possible worlds.

Maggie's bending over the fire. She's about to throw a letter in. Isla catches her.

Mackenzie We all have wur excuses. Eh Lord?

Isla No.

Maggie The fright.

Isla grabs her wrist.

Mackenzie What's yours?

Isla Give me that.

Maggie I've had about enough of you.

Isla You've been burning them.

Maggie For the best.

Isla My letters.

Maggie I did it . . .

Isla How many?

Maggie . . . for the best.

Isla How many?

Maggie It was your Faither that started it.

Isla My letters. (*She sits at the table.*)

Maggie Aye well.

Isla reads the letter. Mackenzie stands at the table with her. Not there.

Mackenzie

Isla,
Not so bad here. Not so very bad. They feed me that's
the main thing. I like my food. I'm to get out soon. Back
on the ships. Back on the convoys. Russia they say. I
want to ask. Would it be a cheek to ask. Can I see you? I
have to ask, can I please see you? I've written an' I've
written. You called the wee lad Grant. That's a fair good
name. Your Mother wrote to me. She says he'll carry
that name. The folks he's gone to. They'll give him that
name. My poor, poor Isla. Let me see you. Forgive me.
    Cath came the once. Sweet Cath. Let her vile tongue
wag at me. Claimed I had my just deserts. What I did I
did out of love for you . . . Don't you hate me now. I
couldn't stand that. Look at me. I'm a poor thing. I'm

not worth your hatred. A frightened man. That's all I am.

At some future time. I'll let you know when I'm out. When I get leave. Where I'll be. I need to know you forgive me. My love goes to you for ever and always.

Isla scrunches up the letter and throws it on the fire. Puts on a jacket, picks up a bag and walks out. Blackout.

THE WINTER GUEST

For Alan Rickman

in memory of
Helen Sinclair Robertson Smith
1912–1993

Characters

Elspeth
Lily
Chloe
Tom
Sam
Frances
Nita
Alex

The **Winter Guest** was first performed at the West Yorkshire Playhouse Courtyard Theatre on 23 January 1995. The cast was as follows:

Elspeth Phyllida Law
Frances Sian Thomas
Alex Christian Zanone
Nita Arlene Cockburn
Tom John Wark/David Evans
Sam John-Ross Morland/Anthony O'Donnell
Chloe Sandra Voe
Lily Sheila Reid

Directed by Alan Rickman
Designed by Robin Day
Music by Michael Kamen
Lighting by Peter Mumford

Act One

Elspeth Call that fox?

Up on the landing, **Elspeth,** *looking through the telescope. Peering. Bent. Concentrated.*

Fox!

Bright sun shining on black-clad ladies at a bus stop. **Lily,** *little fat hands in tight black skin gloves rustling a too big newspaper.* **Chloe,** *neck upstretched, all wrapped around with a black fur tippet, seen better days. Neck craning, dewlap, looking for bus.*

Dyed rabbit. Died long ago that. Catch me in that. Fox? Wants burying that's what that wants. Bury her with it. Face on her. What's she done to get a face like that?

Lily I'm telling you.

Chloe Cream?

Lily There wasn't any.

Chloe Och your face and parsley.

Elspeth is talking to one of the photographs.

Elspeth Don't you look at me like that. (*Turns it to the wall.*) There. Serves you right.

A sound of water splashing darts her back to the telescope.

Lily Did you have a fridge?

Chloe Did we have a fridge?

Lily Did you?

Chloe The rich had refrigerators Lily, that's who the refrigerators belonged to. Good money, we had. We worked for our money. A fridge? Of course we didn't have a fridge.

Lily There you are, then.

Chloe What?

Lily No fridge, no cream.

Chloe Eh?

Lily You need a refrigerator for cream, Chloe. And that's a fact.

Chloe I'll tell you what you need for cream Lily. You need a cow for cream, Lily, that's what you need.

Lily Eh?

Chloe A cow, Lily!

Lily I'm always glad to learn something Chloe.

The newspaper rustles.

Chloe My mother used to make trifles.

Lily Your mother's trifles!

Chloe What?

Lily Custard.

Chloe Custard?

Lily Custard permeated your house, Chloe, the smell of it. Curtains minging with it. Pears in custard. Apple pie. Spotted dick with custard, Chloe. Your mother? Custard in the trifles!

Chloe Thick cream!

The newspaper rustles.

Whipped cream! And I remember the fork that she whipped it with.

Lily After the Second War. That's when there was fridges. That's when there was cream. After rationing. Suez there was cream. I remember a meringue in Jenners Tea Room. 1956, that's when there was cream, I'm telling you.

Chloe You had milk I suppose?

Lily Eh?

Chloe You drank milk.

Lily Of course we drank milk, Chloe. Don't be so damn stupid.

Chloe And where did you keep it?

Lily In a brown clay jug, in the larder, all wrapped around with a cold wet cloth.

Chloe And that's where you kept the cream. In a smaller jug right by its very side. I'm telling you.

The paper rustles and rustles in high indignation.

There's boys running.

Tom Osric Tentacles!

Sam Techno!

Tom Erpland.

Sam You can't like Techno.

Tom Grunge is dead.

Sam Fucking Techno!

He leaps on to a prom horse. Tom takes the other.

Race you.

Tom Jurassic Shift.

Sam Race you.

The creak of prom horses fills the cold morning. The sun gleams bright. Enfolds **Tom** *and* **Sam** *in its light. Tom and Sam working the horses. School-bags dumped in the snow.*

Lily They want oiled.

Chloe Put down. That's what they want. Gun to the head. Kindest in the long run.

Lily Boys.

Chloe I'm cold.

Elspeth Boys.

A distant piano on the edge of hearing. A bored piano, playing the same tune over and over. The boys are much too big for the horses, competing to see who can touch the ground first.

Elspeth Red cheeks. Monkeys.

Sam Hup. Hup.

Tom Get on with you. (*working and working the horses*)

Sam Touching. (*Still working the horses.*)

Tom Bloody isn't.

Sam Bloody touching.

Tom It's not bloody touching.

Sam slides down from the moving horse, picks up his bag and wallops Tom with it.

Sam Wanker.

Knocks Tom off the horse. Runs. Tom runs after him.

Tom Come here you. Sam. You.

Over the rail. Down on to the beach and away. The horses creak. To and fro. To and fro. The distant piano playing.

Elspeth stands back from the telescope. Sun streams through the window. Sings.

Elspeth O can ye wash a sailor's shirt. (*Calls out to the bathroom door.*) There's someone at the piano, cherub. Can you hear? (*Sings*) O can ye wash a sailor's shirt. And hang it on the green. (*To the door.*) Summer music that. Do you hear that piano, Frances? Frances?

Frances I hear it.

Elspeth Summer music.

Frances Yes.

Elspeth Boarding-house music don't you think? Frances?

Frances Yes.

Elspeth D'you mind Prestwick, cherub? And the food in the place. 'The Farmer's Boy' we had over and over. (*Sings.*)

'. . . to be a Farmer's Boy
Thing thing thing.'

They stuffed you. The food. You couldn't move. Fine food. We were all sick when we got back that year. D'you mind that cherub? It was our livers it got to. Paté de fois gras. That's what we were. Stuffed to bursting. And the heat and the thunder storms. Never a breeze that year. And the tide come galloping in. Cherub? Frances?

Frances I'm washing my hair.

Elspeth And the beauty competition. Oh, Frances. Miss Prestwick Junior. I was proud. Your round wee tummy and your round wee bottom. Wiggle, waggle, wiggle, waggling. And you beat that Lynn. I never liked a blonde. What do folk see in blondes, Frances? You never know if it's real. I don't. Frances? What's real, eh? What's real nowadays? Bottoms, busts, lips even. Eyes. (*She stretches her own face out so that the wrinkles disappear.*) Not that I blame them. I don't blame them. Frances?

Frances I can't hear you.

Elspeth Walking round the swimming pool on that man's arm for all the world to see. Parading. In your bubbly red swimsuit and your hair all the way to your wee bahoochey and your prize in your arms. A doll it was. Am I not right? A Mammy doll. Waggling your bottom like a grown-up beauty queen. I could have run down there; I could have bitten it for you, that bottom. I could, I could so. A good hard bite. The lovely smile on your face. You always had a smile. And all the folk looking. I knew. I knew then that you were blest. Blest in all the world. Lucky Frances. Lucky for life and I was too that I had you. Lucky.

Pause. Murmurs.

Touch wood when you say that. Throw salt over your shoulder. 'O can ye wash a sailor's shirt.'

Frances I can't hear you.

Elspeth And your picture in the paper.

Frances What?

Elspeth I have it yet. Don't you worry.

Silence.

What is it cherub?

No reply.

Frances?

No reply. She goes back to the telescope. Swings the telescope. Catches **Nita**. *She's snow carving with a razor shell, down below the prom, on the beach at the edge of the sea. Sculpting a snowman.*

Nice legs. There's a face. Ttt, ttt, ttt.

Nita shades her eyes in the sunlight. Sees **Alex** *wheeling his bike. Nita throws a snowball.*

Alex Hey.

Nita What?

Alex You.

Nita Me?

Alex D'you throw that?

Nita What?

Alex Snowball.

Nita What?

He shrugs. Gets on his bike. She runs to the prom rail.

You'll never ride it.

Alex Sorry?

Nita You'll never ride that.

Alex Is that right?

Nita Mind the ruts.

Alex rides. The chain comes off. Alex's feet go round

and round on nothing. The bike tips. Alex leaps. The bike falls. Alex skids on the frozen snow. Falls.

Alex Shit.

Nita's laughing. She climbs over the prom rail. Watches Alex turn the bike up. Watches him fiddle.

Nita Want a hand?

Alex I'm fine.

She kneels beside him. The chain won't go.

Shit.

Nita Here. (*She loops the chain on.*) Small cog first. (*She grins up at him. Face lifted in the sun.*) What are you looking at?

Elspeth It wants that face. (*She's at the telescope. She's watching Alex.*) Alex. Oh now. Now, now, now. You be careful. (*Watching both of them.*) What does it want, eh? What will it get? Mind yourself cherub. Never be enough for that face, Alex. Nothing's enough for that face. It'll eat you up. Gobble you down. And when it's finished it'll walk away. Leave you an empty shell. You mind. Want, want, want, a face like that. Ah we all want. I want. I've always wanted. I'm wanting yet.

Alex I can fix my own chain.

Nita Oh well. (*She starts to take it off again.*)

Alex Don't take it off. Hey!

Nita You can fix it, you said.

Alex Leave the bloody thing. (*He catches her hand.*) I said leave it. What's your name?

Nita Nita.

Alex Eh?

Nita Nita, for God's Sake.

Pause.

You've got my hand.

Alex I don't know you. I've never seen you before in my life. Have I?

Nita Look.

Alex What?

Nita Who's that? (*He looks up at the window.*)

Alex My gran.

Nita You've still got my hand.

He waves.

Elspeth jumps away from the telescope.

Elspeth Dear, dear, dear. (*Shouts through to the bathroom.*) I'll make the bed, cherub.

Frances What?

Elspeth I'm making your bed for you.

The piano's playing 'Beautiful Dreamer'. A clarinet joins. Nita slides through the prom rails on to the beach. Alex wheels the bike. Stops. Watches Nita. She's back at the snowman carving. Elspeth's leaning at the bedroom door.

Elspeth Listen Frances. Listen cherub. D'you hear that? (*She sings.*)

'I'm good for nothing but to obey your commands.'
(*goes on singing*)
And on the prom. Lily sings.

Lily

Beautiful Dreamer
La, la, la, la.
La, la, la, la, la, la, la, la, la, la, la.

Chloe There's no bus coming. There's none in sight.

Lily La, la, la, la, la.

Chloe What?

Lily Do you not hear it?

Chloe You're in public.

Lily Listen.

Chloe shivers.

What's wrong with you?

Chloe I'm cold, that's all.

Lily Stamp your feet then.

Chloe There's nothing wrong with my feet.

Lily Listen. Listen. It's beautiful.

Chloe Singing in the street. Like you were a wain, Lily.
Where's your dignity?

The piano stops.

Lily There. Pity. That tree's bare of berries.

Chloe I never liked a holly tree.

Lily Redwings, God bless them.

Chloe Terrible cruel things holly trees. Lay me to rest
under a holly tree and I'll come back and haunt you.

Lily You've a long way to go before that.

Chloe Not so long as I've been.

Lily Redwings in from Siberia. Redwings have stripped it bare. Bad weather to come.

Chloe What do you call this then?

Lily Worse to come.

Chloe I don't need any redwings to tell me that. My bones tell me that. My chilblains tell me that. Look at these feet. You look at them, Lily. I used to dance on these feet. I was a good dancer. Look at these shoes.

Lily Very nice.

Chloe I remember shoes.

Lily I remember buses.

Chloe I mean shoes. Shoes with buckles. Shoes with straps. Pointy-toed shoes. Shoes with heels that tapped and clicked when you walked down a tiled hall. Shoes that said, 'Here I am.' 'Make way I'm coming.' Look at these shoes. I've still got dancing in me.

Lily No one to dance with.

Chloe Eh?

Lily Good bit leather.

Chloe I used to shave my eyebrows.

Pause.

Catch your death standing here. Catch your death before you'll catch a bus. (*She shivers.*) Cuts through you. Cuts you in two. (*She nods at the paper.*) Anyone we know?

Lily No. No I don't think so. Not yet.

Chloe Pity.

Lily Oh Chloe.

A great rattling and rustling. A shaking and a crackling.

Chloe What?

Lily 'Peacefully at home.'

Chloe Who?

Lily Guess.

Chloe Tell me. (*Chloe peers over Lily's shoulder.*)

Lily I'm not telling you. (*Lily snatches the paper away.*) 'Will be remembered.' What will she be remembered for? Eh? You answer me that.

Chloe That's my paper. (*She snatches at it.*)

Lily Ah ah ah. (*Lily pulls it away.*)

Chloe Give it to me.

Lily Don't be a spoilsport. A wee bit fun, Chloe. Guess. Go on Chloe. Please.

Pause.

Chloe Do I get the age?

Lily A February birthday, I'll give you that.

Chloe Aquarius.

Lily A February birthday, a February death. I like that. Nice and round.

Chloe I don't know who it was. (*She snatches the paper.*) Where? Where is it?

Lily There.

Chloe Well, well, well, well, well.

Pause.

She'll be remembered. I'll say she'll be remembered.

Lily Last saw her in Skinners. That's where we last saw her. Eating a meringue. Chocolate meringue.

Chloe Was that last week? Or was it the week before?

Lily Looked yellow.

Chloe The meringue?

Lily Not the meringue, Chloe. She looked a bit yellow. You commented.

Chloe But healthy.

Lily Have to be healthy to eat Skinners' meringues. Give you hepatitis. Cream. Stomach of cast iron for these meringues.

Chloe Died healthy then. This cold'll take a few.

Lily So it will.

Chloe Carry a few off.

Lily A good few.

Chloe We'll be busy. Spoilt for choice.

Lily Funeral's on Thursday. Are we free?

Chloe Today we've got. Wednesday we've got.

Lily We'll mark Thursday in then. No flowers.

Chloe Pity. I like a nice floral tribute. No one thinks of the mourners.

Lily Guess what I'm thinking of.

Chloe What?

Lily Guess!

Chloe The workings of your mind are a mystery to me, Lily.

Lily You're acid today, Chloe, acid.

Pause.

I'm thinking of a French cake. That's what I'm thinking of. Pink icing. Will we have a French cake in the town? Today. After? It's a cremation after all. We'll need a treat.

Chloe I've seen many a nice cremation.

Lily It's not as final, Chloe. There's nothing like watching a coffin slip down into the earth. And the soil thudding down on the wood. That's a rare treat these days. Factory death we get these days. All this conservation. All this ecology. You'd think they'd want to save on the gas. That's what I'd think. And the coffins. Profligate. For all you know, when that curtain closes and the coffin goes down the shute, for all we know any of us as regards the body, it might just lift the lid, get up and walk off into another life. 'Fooled you,' it might be saying. You know where you are with a burial. Permanent, a burial. Will we go to Skinners then? Will we?

Pause.

Bite off the top and lick out the cream.

Chloe Call that cream.

Lily Eh?

Chloe T'isn't real cream. Not in the French cakes.

Lily A wee savoury? In the town. A nice Welsh rarebit. A wee poached egg on toast with pepper on. Yellow douk running. After all we've got our bus passes.

Chloe Much good may they do us.

Lily Eh?

Chloe There's no damn bus.

Tom chases Sam on to the prom.

Tom You cussed my mother.

Sam I never.

Tom You cussed her.

Sam Fuck off.

The boys tangle with Chloe. Snow goes down her neck.

Chloe Oh my God! (*Chloe makes to go for them. Lily pulls her back.*)

Lily Hold your horses.

Chloe Getting my hopes up. Think before you speak, Lily. I'll thank you to do that.

Lily I'm sorry.

Tom Come on. Hit me. Hit me. Come on.

Tom's squaring up to Sam.

Chloe I'll hit him alright. Mall boys for goodness sake. It's not as if they're Broughton. Disgrace to the uniform.

Lily It was an accident.

Chloe I've snow right down my neck. I'd like to get hold of his mother. I'd give her what for.

Sam doesn't take Tom on.

Tom Fuck off yourself then.

Sam runs down on to the beach. Tom throws a wild snowball after him. Lily's brushing Chloe down.

Lily Got the wind in their tails.

Chloe I'll give them wind. There's snow trickling right down me. I'm not telling you where that snow's got.

Boys run off knocking Nita's snowman.

Nita You wee sods look what you've bloody well done. (*She makes to go for them.*)

Sam Canny throw for toffee.

Tom Fuck off.

Sam and Tom run along the beach.

Alex It's a snowman. That's all. A bloody snowman.

Nita I don't care. I'm gonnie murder them, the buggers.

Alex Let them be.

Nita It's my snowman.

Alex Leave them alone.

Nita Look at him.

Alex Doesn't matter.

Nita I wanted him perfect.

Alex For fuck's sake. A snowman.

Nita I thought you'd gone.

Alex I came back.

Nita What for? (*She looks at him.*) Come out on the ice with me.

Pause.

Alex Five to nine.

Nita Come out on the ice. Come on. Come on. Come out now. Won't wait. I'm going to do what I want. Just for today, this one day. Exactly what I want. To know what it feels like. Come on to the ice.

Alex What about what I want.

Nita There'll be no one in school. No one at all. Have you seen a bus? There's no buses. There won't be a bus. Not if I don't want one. There are no buses anywhere. Not ever again. And there's only this day left to us out of all our lives. Come out on the ice.

Alex We'll drown out there.

Nita You can swim can't you? (*As Alex steps off rock she drags him down to the edge of the frozen sea.*)

Lily Suck on a peppermint.

Chloe Eh?

Lily An extra strong mint. Keep you warm.

Chloe Have you got one?

Lily searches in her bag.

Lily I haven't.

Chloe You haven't?

Lily I haven't.

Chloe You haven't got a peppermint?

Lily I'm sorry.

Chloe Getting my hopes up. Think before you speak, Lily. I'll thank you to do that.

Lily I'm sorry.

Chloe Easy enough said. Sorry. Doesn't make it better. It's the expectation. An extra strong mint. I'm salivating. Look at those clouds. I hate to be late. Bad manners to be late. We'll miss going past the flower man. We'll miss the flower man when he doffs his hat.

Lily He won't be there.

Chloe He's always there.

Lily In this weather?

Chloe Will we walk?

Lily The old days with them walking in front. That's what I liked.

Chloe The dancing days.

Lily Hardly dancing. Hardly at funerals.

Chloe No such thing as funerals then. No one died then.

Nita and Alex are at the edge of the sea.

Nita Are you scared?

Alex Are you?

Nita Course I am. Feel it. Feel the fear running up and down your back. Cold fingers on your vertebrae. (*She holds out her hand.*) Hold hands.

Alex Come on. (*Grabs her. Hauls her up the beach.*) Yeeeeeeeeeeeees! (*Runs her down on to the ice. Stops.*) Tiptoe.

Frances opens the bathroom door. Comes out into the hall. Towel round her.

Elspeth Oh my God.

Frances rubs her hand over her shorn locks.

Frances The man who led me round that pool was a ballocks. The bathing suit rubbed my nipples raw. The tops of my thighs chapped on the elastic. My right nipple has a bit off the tip because of that bathing suit. When we got back to the boarding house we had egg for tea. You made me eat the white because of India's starving millions.

And I spewed up. The boarding-house woman was blazing because I didn't get to the bathroom and all the sick went down the cracks in her linoleum. You put me to bed and there was a thunderstorm. You have a very selective memory, Mother.

Elspeth What have you done? What have you done to your hair? Oh Frances. Your lovely hair. Cherub, what have you done?

Frances Cut it.

Elspeth I can see that. That's plain to see.

Frances Needed a change.

Elspeth Oh God.

Frances Don't you like it?

Elspeth Your beautiful hair.

Frances A trim, that's all.

Elspeth Is that what you call it?

Frances It'll grow.

Elspeth Did you pay someone to do that to you?

Frances Boyish don't you think?

Elspeth Mannish.

Frances Gives me cheekbones.

Elspeth Are you depressed?

Frances I like it.

Elspeth Doesn't make you look any younger.

Frances The time has come for me to embrace my years, don't you think mother? Welcome them. Not fight them any more.

Elspeth Don't talk nonsense. Why should you embrace your years, no one else does. Anything to be different, Frances. You were the same when you were a wee girl. It's the kingdom of youth that we're living in Frances. I never thought I'd see you let yourself go. No matter what's happened to you. Never give in. Is it your work?

Pause.

Frances Say something nice, mother. Try.

Elspeth You've always had good bone structure. You get that from me. I'll make a beautiful skeleton when my time comes. Makes your neck longer. Very handsome.

Frances Thank you.

Pause.

Elspeth The trouble I used to take over your hair. I used to rub it with silk, make it shine. A Japanese silk scarf. And you'd tell me things. Secrets we had between us. Oh Frances. Those were good days. Have you kept it?

Frances What?

Elspeth Your hair.

Frances No.

Elspeth I mean if you were going to a hot country. (*She looks at her daughter.*) Didn't they give it to you?

Frances I didn't ask.

Elspeth I'd've liked it. Did you never think of that? To keep. Did you never think of me? Of course you didn't. When have you ever, ever, ever thought of me? Maybe they've still got it.

Frances Be in a wig by now.

Elspeth Have you been out like that?

Pause.

What does Alex say?

Frances He likes it.

Elspeth He'd say that. He'd say that to keep you happy.
You've taught that lad well.

Frances goes down the hall.

Wear some earrings for God's sake. Let folk know you're a
woman.

Frances goes into the bedroom.

Long earrings.

Frances shuts the bedroom door.

Are you going to a hot country? Is that why you cut it?
(*She turns the photograph round.*) I blame you for this.
My God. (*Elspeth goes to the telescope. Swivels it. Wipes
her eyes. Looks through it.*)

Sam's chasing Tom. Gets him round the neck.

Tom Get off.

Sam I put the pressure on. I put the pressure on here.
Round by your ear. Feel that, eh? Feel it?

Tom I feel it. I feel it.

Sam Know what this is called. Eh? Eh?

Tom No.

Sam Eh?

Tom No.

Sam I can't hear you.

Tom I don't know what it's fucking called.

Sam Want to know?

Tom You're hurting me.

Sam Do you want to know what this is called?

Tom Yes. Yes.

Sam Five seconds and you're dead.

Tom Tell me.

Sam A 'Killer' this is called. A fucking 'Killer'.

Tom Get off. Get off.

Sam I squeeze that's all. One squeeze. Feel that.

Silence.

Do you feel it?

Tom I feel it?

Sam I can't hear you.

Tom Fuck off.

Sam I squeeze. I hold it for five seconds. Pressure point. You're dead at my feet.

Tom shouts.

Tom I feel it.

Sam What?

Tom's yelling at the top of his voice.

Tom I fucking feel it.

Sam I'm counting. One. Two.

Tom Fuck off.

He kicks hard at Sam's legs with his feet. Sam doubles up. Tom runs. Sam flings a snowball after him. Then chases.

Elspeth's telescope lights on Nita and Alex out on the ice.

Alex Far enough.

Nita We can get to the rock.

Alex I'm going back.

Nita Right in the middle on that rock. We'd be surrounded then. In the middle of the ice.

Alex Gets thinner.

Nita Doesn't.

Alex Look at it.

Nita Where?

Alex For God's sake, Nita, you can practically see the fish.

Nita You go back if you want. (*She steps out.*) See.

Alex Christ. (*He jumps after her and goes straight through. Up to his ankles.*) Jesus.

   Nita starts to laugh.

Don't just stand there. It isn't fucking funny, Nita. It's fucking freezing this. (*He steps.*) I could get frostbite.

   The ice breaks.

Jesus. Give me your hand. (*Steps.*) Help me, Nita. I could get gangrene.

Nita You've made a fishing hole.

Alex Fuck off.

Nita Don't be a baby.

Alex People get their limbs cut off. They lose their toes, Nita.

Nita You're nearly on the beach.

Alex There's a bus. There's a bloody bus sitting there. They'll all be in school, Nita. In the warm they'll be, Nita, for Christ sake. (*He wades back to the shore. Crunching the ice down as he goes.*)

Lily Is that not a twenty-six?

Chloe Where?

Lily Sitting there. See its white top. At the terminus, Chloe. Will we run for it?

Chloe My running days are long gone.

Lily You've a fine pair of legs on you.

Chloe Eh?

Lily You've a fine pair of legs on you yet.

Chloe runs a hand up her leg straightening her stocking.

I'm not missing my Monday morning. I've been shut up all weekend. It's a big funeral this and I'm not missing it. I've not been to a big one since I don't know when. Since his. Since his up there. (*She's pointing up to Frances' house.*) And it's a young one. His was the last young one.

Chloe Wasn't that young?

Lily Forty, Chloe. Young to you and me.

Chloe They have a look of death about them the ones that are going to go young. About the mouth, about the eyes.

Lily He was a very handsome man.

Chloe A look of fate. A sadness, Lily, you'll not deny that.

Lily I'm going, Chloe. I'll achieve something this day. You'll come or not come as you see fit. With or without you Chloe. That's my bus.

Chloe In all this wind? Could we not go home? We could light a fire.

Lily At this time of day.

Chloe We could be profligate just this once.

Lily I thought you wanted to go.

Chloe I do.

Lily Well then. Warm you up. Do you good.

Chloe Do me in more like. (*She's off.*)

Lily Chloe.

Chloe D'you want it to go without us?

Lily Off like the March wind. Running like a spring chicken. Chloe!

Alex has reached the shore. He's taking off his shoes and socks.

Nita It's not my fault.

  Alex is hopping about.

You could sit down.

Alex Where do you come from?

Nita I live up on the hill.

Alex That's nice for you. You'll have a sea view. (*He glares at her.*)

Nita Here. (*She holds out her hand.*)

Alex What?

Nita Hold on to me?

Alex Don't you bloody touch me.

Nita Come on.

Alex´ Get away from me. (*He falls over. She's laughing at him.*)

Nita You only went in up to your ankles. It's not the end of the world.

> *He catches hold of her. Pulls her down. Rubs the snow on her.*

Alex If I'm going to freeze to death, you can bloody freeze to death.

Elspeth Be kissing next.

> *Alex lets go of Nita.*

I'd have had him kissing. Been me. In my young day, behind the bandstand. He'd have kissed me alright. Missed her chance.

Nita You're late.

Alex I don't care. Jesus Christ.

Nita What?

Alex My feet are dropping off.

Nita Go and get a dry pair of socks for God's sake.

Alex My grandmother's in there. My mother's had her hair cut. That's a bloody battlefield.

Frances powers out of the bedroom. She has a handful of photographs in her hand.

Elspeth What are these? What are they?

Frances Have a look.

Elspeth Did you take these?

Frances For a school prospectus.

Elspeth Buildings?

Frances With the big camera.

Elspeth The one I bought you?

Frances Yes. Yes. Thank you for that.

Elspeth Make it sound like a curse. Why is it so hard?

Frances What?

Elspeth Is saying thank you so hard?

Frances Without the camera you bought me I couldn't have taken this job.

Elspeth I thought you'd take people. That's what I thought you wanted it for. People, that's why I bought it.

Frances What's wrong with them?

Elspeth Have you nothing exciting to show me?

   Pause.

Frances You don't have to keep checking up on me.

Elspeth Do I not?

Frances I'm alright?

Elspeth Look at you.

Frances I don't need you.

Elspeth Don't you ever say that to me.

   Her hands are out of control. Gesturing. Till Frances catches hold of them. Holds them tight.

Looking after a person, being responsible for them. That's hard learnt. I was a young woman when I had you with a young woman's preoccupations. You taught me to care,

my God. Demanded that I . . . that I care. With your
screaming and your crying and your wee hands that beat
at me and grabbed at me. You taught me to look after you
twenty-four hours of the day. That's what you taught me.
Step by step by step. You cut me out of my old life and
then you kept me from it. Step by step the two of us went.
So. What do you expect? Just because you're all grown up.
I've to stop? All that caring. I've to stop? To know you're
alright.

Frances I'm fine.

Elspeth You don't look fine.

Frances I'm not sick.

Elspeth I want the best for you.

   The hands escape.

That's all I want. All I've ever wanted. Frances. Cherub.

Frances I like these. Look. These.

Elspeth Better you have it now. Better you get it now than
the tax man when I die. Better I see you get the pleasure
out of . . .

Frances I'll pay you back.

Elspeth Better you have it now than when I'm in my box.

Frances That's the school. See. See.

Elspeth I hated school. My work years they were the best
years. I'd be working yet.

Frances I love this one.

Elspeth Do you?

Frances Look at the movement in it.

Elspeth If you want movement, Frances, make a film.

Frances They're not the final prints. Look. Look at this paper. I'm trying out different papers. Look at this, Mother. The depth you get in this.

Elspeth Snaps for a school prospectus. They'll never hang in the Tate.

Frances This is old, this paper. Camera shop man, he gave it to me.

Elspeth What age is he?

Frances I couldn't afford to buy it.

Elspeth Is he married?

Frances The grain on it.

Elspeth He must like you to give you all that.

Frances I'm not looking for a husband.

Elspeth You can't live alone.

Frances I've Alex.

Elspeth You're still a young . . . Cutting your hair.

Frances See this.

Elspeth It's damn lonely living on your own. I know that. I like a colour picture.

Frances Here. Here.

Elspeth Why do you not use colour? The world's in colour, cherub.

Frances Why don't you just come out and say it. You don't like them, do you?

Elspeth It's not me you have to please.

Frances I please myself.

Elspeth Nonsense.

Frances I do what I want.

Elspeth Nonsense.

Frances I do.

Elspeth Have it your own way.

   Pause. She holds out the photographs.

Congratulations.

Frances Thank you.

Elspeth A man could have taken these. There. Does that suit you?

Frances I'm not quite sure.

Elspeth Your hair and your work. You're all of a piece now.

Frances What?

Elspeth I don't see you in these pictures.

Frances I'm proud of them.

Elspeth Are you?

Frances Work's pouring in. The phone never stops ringing.

   Silence.

Elspeth Well that's nice. That's very nice.

Frances Jesus, Mother.

Elspeth Show me a photograph you wanted to take.

Frances I'm paid to take those.

Elspeth Compromise. Every last one.

Frances Don't talk rot.

Elspeth A happy woman doesn't mutilate herself. I'm not talking about the husband that you lost. A woman that's happy in her work. A woman that's happy in her home. A happy woman doesn't ruin her own beauty.

Frances You don't know what you're looking at.

Elspeth Don't I?

Frances This is my body and I can do what I like with it. I can get fat if I like. I can cut my own hair. I happen to think I look good.

Elspeth I've seen you look better.

Frances Come on.

Elspeth I've seen better photographs. These are better photographs. Every last one of them. You photographed a death and it dried you up.

Frances Will we go shopping, will we? Your shopping, Mother.

Elspeth They're pedestrian that's what they are. Tell me about your light and your shade and your edge. Tell me about it. Your depth. Where's the risk? Show me one picture. One picture that you wanted to take.

Frances sorts through the bundle.

Frances I'm a good technician. I learn with every picture that I take.

Elspeth I'm all for learning.

Frances Here . . .

Elspeth That's Alex.

Frances I don't expect you to like it.

Elspeth I can see your hand in this. That's Australia.

Frances You like it?

Elspeth Maybe he'll have a chance now.

Frances What are you talking about?

Elspeth Don't you play the innocent. You had room for no one else in your life, the two of you.

Frances You're trespassing, Mother.

Elspeth I'm scared to death.

Frances I'm warning you.

Elspeth No room for that boy in your lives. Don't you walk away from me. As well he's dead. There. I'll say what has to be said. You were obsessed the two of you. You're obsessed yet. (*She takes a picture down.*)

Frances Give it to me.

    Pause.

Give it to me.

Elspeth Days passing in a dream. He lives in your dreams now. Don't you tell me. Days lost. Weeks. And then you'll look. Years'll be gone. Years will have passed from out of your grasp. And you'll wonder where they've gone to. One life, that's all. You'll not get the lost years back.

Frances It was dark blue that raincoat.

    Elspeth taps the photograph of Alex.

Elspeth Here. Here.

Frances The Barrier Reef.

Elspeth I know that.

Frances D'you like it?

Elspeth Do you want to go back there?

Frances Where's your stick?

Elspeth I can walk without a stick. Do you want to go back to Australia?

Frances Where is it?

Elspeth I didn't bring it. You're not answering me. You liked Australia, didn't you?

Frances I wasn't there that long. Did you walk along here without a stick?

Elspeth I did.

Frances In the snow?

Elspeth They didn't clear a path in front of me.

Frances You're a fool, Mother.

Elspeth I thought I did rather well.

Frances You could have killed yourself.

Elspeth I can do without a stick. I'm getting better.

Frances runs down the stairs.

Frances I've an umbrella here that you can use.

Elspeth You can keep it.

Frances Mother.

Elspeth I'm not using your umbrella. I don't like it.

Frances What's wrong with it?

Elspeth There's a lot of things I don't like that you have. That you do. I keep quiet about it.

Frances When are you ever quiet?

Elspeth Was it sex you and yon dead man. Was that what it was?

199

Frances Take the umbrella.

Elspeth I'll do things my own way. Or I'll not do them at all. (*She turns her back on Frances.*) I don't want you to take me to do my shopping. I don't need you.

Frances I'm to sit at home am I and wait for casualty to call?

Elspeth I'm getting better.

Frances It's alright for you to tell me what to do. That's alright is it?

Elspeth Why do you hate me?

Frances Jesus.

Elspeth You always loved your father best.

Frances Please.

Elspeth Don't you think I didn't know. Girls and their fathers.

Frances Where's the tears, Mother?

Elspeth Are you going back to Australia?

Frances No tears?

Elspeth I need a drink to cry. A half-bottle of Gordon's, then I'll cry. I'll cry alright. Gin tears. The only sort I've got left. My tear ducts have dried up. It's only the gin that can make me lachrymose.

   Frances laughs.

Let me try without the stick Frances. I hate the stick. If I fall, you're there.

Frances Not always.

Elspeth I don't like shops. I don't like shopping.

Frances You have to eat tomorrow.

Elspeth Bugger tomorrow, Frances. I'm not talking about tomorrow. You're with me today and we could have fun. You were a wee girl. Remember this. Remember. 'Let's walk.' And off we'd go. Just the two of us. Staring into folk's houses to see their different lives. 'I'll live there when I grow up.' 'Look at those curtains.' I'd have hot chocolate. You'd have lemonade. Sugar in to fizz it up. Am I sentimental? Am I? Bugger it you can let me. Folk would stare at us. You've got their faces on now, Frances. Lethargic. Maybe we both have. Maybe it's winter that does it. Crayons you'd buy. Or pencils. Nothing much. 'Look. Look at that dress. I wouldn't wear that. I wouldn't put that on my back.'

'I want to be her.' 'I want her smile.'

Frances 'I want her cake.' 'I want her shoes.' (*She's laughing.*)

Elspeth I want her man.

Pause.

You think it'll last for ever. That's what you think. Like the long summer holidays. My year started in September when you were young. Climbed up the hill to Christmas. Roller-coaster ride to spring. I know we fought. Near scratched each other's eyes out. I like a fight. No stick, Frances. Just this day. No umbrella. I like a bright umbrella. I must have brightness in my life. Look at your hair, Frances.

Frances It's growing.

Elspeth Not fast enough. Did you like Australia?

Frances Yes.

Elspeth Did you?

Frances Yes.

Elspeth And Alex? (*The photograph.*) Alex looks happy.

Frances He'd live there if he could.

Elspeth Look at the day it is. Bugger the shops. Bugger them. Take your camera and we'll go out. Take your camera. And I'll be with you. I'll be quiet Frances. Take me out to work with you. I'd like to watch you work. I'd like that, Frances. I'd like that very much.

Frances It's freezing out there.

Elspeth I can put a jumper on. I've my fur coat. You've a jumper you can lend me. Please, Frances. Please.

On the beach.
The boys.

Tom Any cigs?

Sam No.

Tom Neither me. I've a Mars Bar.

Sam Wanker.

  Silence.

Tom Want a bit? Half and half.

  Sam shrugs.

King size Mars Bar.

Sam Half and half?

Tom Uh huh.

Sam Gonnie measure it?

Tom Got a ruler?

Sam Uh huh.

Tom gets out a book, lays it flat on the beach. Sam's got the ruler out.

Tom Give us it. (*He measures the Mars Bar.*) Fifteen centimetres.

Sam Seven and a half. Mark it.

Tom Got a knife?

Sam I'll cut it.

Tom My Mars Bar.

Sam My knife.

Tom Show us.

Sam brings out a Swiss Army knife.

Bloody Hell. Crockett sees that, he'll do you.

Sam Crockett's not gonnie see it.

Tom Chucked Shanks out for carrying a knife.

Sam Wanker Shanks was. I'm not gonnie use the fucking thing. Crockett's a wanker. Gonnie tell him?

Tom I cut the Mars Bar.

Sam Crockett's a pouf.

Pause. Sam throws him the knife.

Seven and a half mind.

Tom opens the knife.

Tom Good knife. (*Tom cuts the Mars Bar.*)

Sam My mouth's watering.

Tom throws Sam the knife. Holds out the Mars Bar.

Chuck it then.

Tom Closer we sit together, warmer we'll be.

Sam You a pouf?

Tom D'you want this?

Sam Wanker. (*But he comes in close. The pair of them sit on their bags. Tear back paper. Munch on the bar.*)

Up in the house. Jumpers are flying out of the bedroom on to the landing.

Elspeth My God Frances. What's this? The colours in this. This is the one I'll have.

The jumpers keep on flying.

Comes down to my knees Frances. Stop. Stop.

Frances comes out of the room.

What do I look like?

Frances Fine.

Elspeth is at the mirror.

Elspeth Is that my face?

Frances You look great.

Elspeth You should change on the inside, do you know that? That would be fairer. Change on the inside keep up with the outside. I get a fright when I look in the mirror. I'm the same inside as I was at seventeen. And look at me. Look at me. I hate my old face. Give me a sensible jumper in keeping with my years.

Frances Suits you.

She's holding her mother's coat out for her. Shrugs her into it. Rubs the collar against her mother's face. Elspeth laughs.

Elspeth More. More.

Frances Shouldn't wear fur.

Elspeth Died long ago Frances. Long, long, long ago. Forty years I've had this coat. Waste if I didn't wear it.

The boys, munching on the beach. Nita's watching Alex.

Alex What?

Nita What?

Alex Come here.

Nita What for?

Alex I'm sorry.

Frances and Elspeth come out of the house.

Nita What for?

Alex Come here.

Alex grabs Nita.

Nita What?

Alex Get down.

Nita What the hell? Get down will you? Is that your mum?

Alex She'll see my bike.

Nita She's talking.

Alex Talking to my gran? Sniping more like. Which way are they going?

Nita Lighthouse.

Alex They'll be a while. House is empty. Come home with me?

Pause.

Nita If you like.

As Alex runs back up to join Nita, Sam screams.

Tom What the fuck's up with you?

Nita and Alex leave the beach.

Sam It's a worm. It's a worm.

Tom It's not.

Sam It's a big fat skooshy worm.

Tom You scared of worms?

Sam No.

Tom Ay you are.

Sam Ay I'm not.

Tom Imagine. Scared of a wee worm.

Sam Look at it. It's a squelcher.

Tom It's a condom.

Sam Shit.

Tom It's been used.

Sam I touched that. I fucking touched that. Some wanker put it there and I touched it.

Tom Found one up a tree once.

Sam I touched it.

Tom Six meters up.

Sam I touched it with my hand. I've geek on my fingers.

Tom Up a tree. 'Magine that.

Sam I'm gonnie die.

Tom 'Magine doing it up a tree.

Sam I'm dying from the geek on my fingers.

Tom 'Magine doing it.

Sam Help me God.

Tom Wonder what it's like.

Sam Help me Jesus.

Tom You prayin'?

Sam What if?

Tom You prayin' to God?

Sam I'm prayin' to my Aunt Fanny. What do you think I'm doin'?

Tom Probably didn't do it up a tree. Probably threw it there after. What do you do with them after? Eh? They don't tell you in them films. Bloody films. Call that education. Them people doing it. All fat with plukes? Not everyone's fat with plukes? If it's like that, doing it, like them two in that film, I'm going to be a wanker. I'll be a wanker all my life. It's the only fucking option. If my balls drop. If they ever drop. My balls are never gonnie drop. Ron's balls have dropped to his knees. And Harry. I'm two inches taller than Harry and he's got balls. Emir's had his operated on. They've dropped, twisted, been cut about and they're back in operation. They've lived a life his balls and mine haven't even entered the arena yet. I've got this empty bag of skin between my legs that sticks to my thighs when I get hot. Waiting, just waiting. Emir wears a jockstrap for fuck sake. Peter Allan has a wet dream every night. Jesus Christ help me. Every morning I wake up I leap out of the bed. Down go the boxers. I look. Empty. Dear God help me. Christ Jesus lend us a hand.

Sam's washing his hands in the snow.

Sewage runs down this beach. That snow's got shit in it. You're washing your hands in shit. Won't get a blue flag on this beach, not in a million years. It's sunk deep the shit here, years and years and years of it. Heaps of it. These houses are built on it. Never get rid of it. Never, never, never. (*Tom picks up a stick.*)

Sam What you doing?

Tom picks up the condom and inserts the stick. Marches down to the snowman. Sticks the stick in the snowman at groin level.

Tom What a whopper, eh?

Sam Lucky bugger. Wanker, eh?

Tom What would you do with one that size?

Pause.

Sam Hell of a box you'd have to wear.

Tom Eh?

Sam Cricket.

Tom I hate summer.

Pause.

Bloody freezing.

Sam Could light a fire.

Tom You got matches?

Sam Some.

Tom Nothing to burn.

Sam Dry seaweed. Sticks. Rubbish. Plenty about.

Tom Like a fire.

Sam Come on then.

A-gathering they go. Nita and Alex are in the house. Tom shouting.

Tom Need a bloody dump, me.

Sam Go on then.

Tom Where?

Sam There's that much shit on this beach a bit fresh won't make any difference.

Tom I can't.

Sam Dig a hole and bury it that's what a dog'd do.

Tom Cat buries it. Dog doesn't give a shit.

Sam I'd like to be a cat. Cat has a good life.

Tom Fox got our one. Mum won't have another.

Sam You doin' it?

Tom Back of the old bunker.

Sam Still rather be a cat.

Tom Open my bag. See the Maths book.

Sam Uh huh.

Tom Chuck it.

Sam chucks it a long chuck. Sound of tearing paper.

Knew I'd find a use for it.

Sam goes on making a pile of dry seaweed, yellow newspaper, paper wrappers and wood.

Nita's shivering.

Alex What's up.

Nita Freezing in here.

Alex Cold in its bones this house.

Nita Colder in here than it was outside.

Alex Heating's bust.

Nita Can't you get it fixed.

Alex Been bust for ages.

   Nita shivers.

I'll warm you up.

   Pause.

D'you want a bath?

Nita What d'you mean?

Alex Hot bath. That'll warm you.

Nita If you don't mind.

Alex Go on.

Nita Sure?

Alex Up there.

Nita Don't forget your feet.

Alex Top of the stairs.

Nita Thank you very much.

Alex Bubble bath. Oil. Submarine. Use what you like.

   Pause.

There's a lock on the door.

Nita These your Dad?

Alex The rest of her pictures are in the studio. Some in the darkroom. Studio's a mess.

Alex watches her. Nita disappears into the bathroom.

One two three four.

The lock snecks in.

Shit. (*Steps forward on frozen feet.*) Shit. (*Tearing off school uniform. Tie, jumper, blazer. Shivering.*) Jesus. (*Shoving on a jumper from the stairs. Kneeling at the fireplace. Striking a match. Lighting the papers rolled up in the fireplace. Opening up the kindling box. Laying sticks on the fire. Breaking some. Holding feet out to the flames, waiting for the sticks to catch.*)

On the beach the boys bring back armfuls of stuff.

Tom Bloody stinks this. (*He throws his stuff down.*) Give us the matches then. Come on.

Sam Won't burn like that.

Tom It'll burn.

Sam There's an art to a fire.

Tom I'm bloody freezing.

Sam puts stones round in a ring. Tom picks up stones, aims them at the snowman's stick. Aims. Throws. Misses. Aims. Throws. Hits the target.

Yeeeeeees. (*Sings.*) Poor bloody snowman's lost his dong, lost his dong, lost his dong. Poor bloody snowman's lost his dong. Where will he find a new one?

Sam That all you can think of?

Pause.

Tom Yup.

Sam lights the match. Some of the fire catches. Sam lights another one. Blows on the flames. Tom's looking down the inside of his trousers.

Sam You could help.

Tom 'M busy.

Pause.

The fire's alight.

Sam looks over Tom's shoulder.

Sam What do you call that?

Pause.

Tom Maggot.

Sam Know what you should do.

Tom What?

Sam Rub some Deep Heat on.

Tom What for?

Sam Make it grow.

Tom How?

Sam Heat.

Tom Eh?

Sam They swell in the heat.

Tom Do they?

Sam Swell in the heat. Shrivel in the cold. Deep Heat makes them grow. Penetrates.

Pause.

Tom Have you got any?

Sam What?

Tom Deep Heat.

Sam Yup.

Tom Where?

Sam In my bag.

Tom Why?

Sam Got it off my brother.

Tom Eh?

Sam He uses it.

Tom On his dong?

Sam Fucking huge one he's got.

Tom Uses Deep Heat?

Sam Probably does. (*He digs out the Deep Heat. An old tube, wrinkled and bent.*)

Tom You tried it?

Sam Not yet.

Tom Going to?

Sam Only got this much. Want it?

Tom D'you?

Sam You can have it.

   He holds it out to Tom. Tom sniffs it.

Tom Jesus.

Sam What?

Tom 'S' at off.

Sam That's the goodness in it.

Tom takes it. Goes on sniffing.

Tom Stench brings tears to your eyes.

Sam It's not your eyes you're using it on. Male strippers put it on.

Tom How do you know?

Sam They need big ones so they use this. That's all the women are interested in. No good having a maggot if you're a male stripper.

Tom I don't want to be a stripper.

Sam Never know when it might come in handy. There's no such thing as security these days. Need to be able to turn your hand to anything. My Dad's an architect. Fucking good one, too. None of your Prince Charles stuff he does. He's got an imagination, my Dad. He's been made redundant. Sits on the sofa, he does. Grey in the face. More than one string to your bow you need. That's what he says. He'd work in a pub. He'd do anything. Take his clothes off if it wouldn't be an obscenity he's so old. Wrinkled balls he's got and a big vein running down his dick. Varicose veins on his dick he's got. Looks like. And piles. Imagine a stripper with piles.

Pause.

Try it. A good dollop.

Tom That's all there is.

Sam Better than nothing.

Tom Will it make my balls drop?

Sam Dunno.

Tom rubs the Deep Heat in.

Put it away. Keep it warm.

Pause.

Tom It's burning a bit.

Sam That's it working.

Tom's wriggling.

Keep still.

Tom Sam.

Sam What?

Tom It's burning.

Sam Bound to, a bit.

Tom Sam.

Sam What?

Tom Sam.

Sam For fuck sake.

Tom It's burning. It's burning. My penis is on fire.

Sam Jesus. Keep your keks up. (*Runs down to the edge of the sea. Grabs some ice.*)

Tom Help my Bob. Help my Bob.

Sam They'll can see.

Tom Help me. Help me. Help me.

Sam Gonnie get yourself arrested.

Tom My dong's falling off.

Sam drops the ice in Tom's pants. Tom screams. Sam zips him into his trousers.

Sam Quiet.

Pause.

Better?

Tom Oh fuck. Oh fuck. Fuck, fuck, fuck. Mammy, Daddy, Mammy, Daddy, fuck, fuck, fuck.

Sam Is it better? Is it? Is it?

Tom Mammy, Daddy, Mammy, Daddy.

Sam Shut up for fuck's sake.

Tom Oh shite, oh shite.

Sam Want me to belt you?

Tom Bugger, bugger, bugger.

Sam I'll belt you if you don't shut up.

Pause.

It was only a wee bit of cream.

Tom You try it. You try it. Just you bloody try it.

Pause.

Sam You cryin'?

Tom Bloody cry if I want to.

Sam passes him a handkerchief.

Sam Has it grown.

Tom Fucking dropped off that's what it's done.

Sam Has it though?

Tom looks.

Tom No.

Sam You look like you've wet yourself.

Tom stands close to the fire.

Wasn't my fault.

Tom doesn't speak.

Could've worked. (*He digs around in his bag.*) Here. (*He's holding a cigarette out to Tom.*)

Tom 'S' at for me.

Sam looks around, shrugs, goes to take it away.

Thought you said . . .

Sam What?

Tom Bloody cigarette. (*Challenge.*)

Sam What did I say?

Pause.

Tom Give it.

Sam passes it over.

Want half?

Sam Naaaa.

Tom Got a match?

Sam Your face an' a . . .

Tom Fuck off.

Sam strikes a match. Tom bends to his hands. Takes a long haul on the cigarette.

Jeeeees . . . us.

Elspeth is standing at the rail on the prom. She takes a silver cigarette case out of her pocket. Takes out a

cigarette. Dunts it on the case. Puts it in her mouth.
Flicks a cigarette lighter. The piano's playing 'Sailor's
Shirt'. Elspeth is singing, watching Frances at the water's
edge.

Elspeth

Oh can ye wash a sailor's shirt
Oh can ye wash it clean
Oh can ye wash a sailor's shirt and hang
  it on the green?

Watching the boys.

Tom Another wanker not at school.

Sam Eh?

Tom Him on the piano. (*Tom takes a long drag on the*
cigarette. Blows out smoke.)

This is good. This is good Sam. This is a good bit. Got to
know the good bits.

The fire burns bright. Flares high. The piano's loud.
Blackout.

Act Two

Piano and clarinet playing 'Beautiful Dreamer'. Flashing light. There's Elspeth in the flashes, sitting on a rock. Posing. The camera clicks and flashes and whirrs. Elspeth crumples into laughter.

Frances Keep still.

Elspeth's laughter grows.

I said . . .

Light flashes. Images of Elspeth laughing. Her hand goes up to her face.

Elspeth Stop.

The camera goes on. Elspeth takes cigarettes and a lighter from her pocket.

I said enough.

Elspeth lights the cigarette. The only light is the cigarette lighter. Sam chucks paper on to the fire. It flares up. He sings. Softly at first. Then a pure clear boy's voice.

Sam

As a white candle in a Holy Place.
So is the beauty of an aged face.
As the spent radiance of the winter sun
So is a woman with her travail done

Elspeth's head turns towards the sound.

Her brood gone from her
And her thoughts as still

As the waters
Under a ruined mill.

Tom Jesus. Where'd you get that?

Sam Choir.

Tom Bit fucking sad isn't it? Bit of a fucking dirge.

Sam I like it.

Tom Have them rolling in the aisles that. Splitting their sides laughing they'll be. Have them howling for more.

Sam Don't sing for them.

Tom Who d'you sing for?

Sam shrugs.

How many things d'you go to?

Sam This 'n that.

Tom How many?

Sam Collegium.

Tom Bullshit.

Sam Choir. Scouts.

Silence.

What? What?

Tom Shit.

The fire's low.

Fire's going down. Need more stuff.

Sam leaps to his feet.

What're you jumping up for. Never at peace.

Sam is off collecting.

Leaping about the place.

Sam Don't sit still too long. You'll freeze to death. (*He's wandering further afield.*) I've my games kit.

Tom Eh?

Sam In my bag. Dry keks.

Tom dives into Sam's bag. Yells after him.

Tom Could've said. Could've bloody said. (*Lays out track-suit trousers. Smooths them. Smells them.*) Clean, for Christ sake. (*Breathes in the smell of them.*) Mammy's boy. (*Rubs them against his cheek.*) Bloody ponce. (*Kicks off shoes and unzips trousers. Takes them off. Pulls his shirt down as far as it will go. Looks around him. Whips off wet knickers. Holds his shirt down. Bends to get the track-suit trousers.*)

Elspeth What are you looking at?

Frances I can look.

Elspeth Not at me. Not like that you can't. Those eyes.

Frances What's wrong with them?

Elspeth Secret eyes.

Frances How do you want me to be?

Elspeth Open.

Frances You shouldn't smoke.

Elspeth I'll do what I like. We're a long time dead. I always had you nice when you were wee. My own clothes cost me nothing. I'd get up. I'd queue in the sales for my clothes. Wee suits. Wee box jackets. Wee grey suits. Six o'clock I'd be standing there. Summer and winter. Pettigrew and Stevens. Flask of coffee. You? You never had a sale garment on your back.

Frances catches hold of her hands.

Frances Don't.

Elspeth What? What is it for God's sake?

Frances Don't wave your hands about.

Elspeth I don't know what's wrong with you. Cherub?

Frances Don't.

Elspeth It's good this that we're doing today.

Frances Yes.

Elspeth Is this not good? Look around you. Are you enjoying yourself? Are you?

Frances Yes, Mother. Yes I am.

Elspeth I'd not have had you hurt. I'd not have seen you crying. You'd have better borne it if I'd died.

Frances Please, Mother.

Elspeth Don't you think I'd have taken his place to save you hurt. I prayed God to take me in his stead.

Frances You were safe enough offering. Doesn't work like that, does it? Does it?

Elspeth My coat's warm. Deep pockets in this coat. I'm in love with my coat, Frances. Feel the air, Cherub. Know where the good bits are. Seize them, Frances. Grab and hold hard. Hold very hard.

Pause.

Look at that fire. I like a beach fire . . . (*She gets up.*)

Tom Bloody prize you are, three-quarters, seven bloody

eighths throwing this away, don't know they're born.

Sparks fray out from the fire in the hall. Alex is poking it.
Nita is out on the top landing at the mirror.

Nita Do you think I look like a boy?

Alex Jesus.

Nita Did I frighten you?

Alex You look nice.

Nita I don't look like a girl though. (*She's got a towel*
round her.)

Alex Eh?

Nita If you cut off my head and stuck it on a pole it'd be a
boy's head. Anybody looking at it. Standing there. That's a
boys head, they'd say. Poor chap. Not just my head.
Further down I could get away with it. Down to my belly
button I could be a boy. I've got boy's knees. (*She runs*
down the stairs.) Look. (*Flops beside him. Exposes one*
knee.) Knobbles. (*She bangs at her knee with her fist.*)

Alex Don't do that.

Nita Feel this. (*Flexes her arm muscles.*) Come on have a
feel of this.

   He does.

Well?

Alex Very nice.

Nita Strong?

Alex Very strong.

Nita Not much of a turn-on.

   Pause.

Alex Take off the towel.

Nita No.

Alex Let's have a look at you.

Nita Don't be daft.

Alex Take off the towel and I'll tell you what you are.

Nita I didn't mean that. (*She crawls over to the lowest jumper on the stairs and slops it on.*)

Alex Nita?

Nita moves away from him. Wanders up the stairs to the telescope. Alex feeds the fire with coal. She's looking through the telescope.

The sun flares down on to Frances and Elspeth.

Elspeth When are you going?

Frances What?

Elspeth Are you going? When are you going? Simple question. I'm not a fool, Frances.

Nita Your Mother's beautiful.

Frances Give me a cigarette.

Elspeth I don't blame you.

Frances Give me one. (*She lights the cigarette.*) Cold?

Elspeth It's a good coat this.

Frances Let me know when you want to go back.

Elspeth Suits me this. My God it's bleak. I love it. Winter. I like weather. Definite weather. When it rains I like it pelting down. Stotting off the pavements, I like it. And the wind. I like a good blow. Sunshine. Couldn't be doing

with it all the time and never a cloud in the sky. Look at
this. Look at it. Clean it up and there's nowhere on this
earth could beat it for beauty. I like the seasons. Autumn's
my beginning. You'll miss the seasons when you go.
Leaves falling. The haar rolling in. It's the weather gets
me up in the morning. There's nothing else I've got to get
up for.

Frances I haven't made up my mind Mother, that's the
truth.

Blue cigarette smoke rises.

Elspeth You tell me. Go on. What have I got to get up for?

Frances Stop it.

Elspeth I get up to fight my body that's what I get up for.
And sometimes I win. For an hour or two I win. A day or
two if I'm lucky. Do you think I look to you? Do you? Do
you think I need you? Do you? I don't need you. There
isn't a living soul that I need. I look at you and I don't
envy you. You make it hard. Living. You. All of you. You
think you're so much better. Dear God. I haven't made
such a mess of it.

Frances puts her hands over her ears. Cigarette in hand.

I don't expect anything from you. I've had little enough
God knows. You could tell me straight. Are you going?
Are you staying? You could pay me that compliment.
Discuss it with me. You're a closed person. A secret
person. When I see what some daughters do for their
mothers. After . . . after what happened to you . . . I
thought we would draw in, draw close. I thought you
might need . . . a person . . . I don't care, Frances, I don't
care who it is. A person needs to be needed. And if you
don't need me, you could . . . you could lie. Frances! If
you're not going to smoke that why did you take it. I

know you're listening. (*Elspeth's cigarette's finished. She gets out another. The lighter flicks.*)

Sam comes to the fire carrying a cardboard box. Calling. The telescope light swings.

Sam Hey.

Tom What the fuck? What've you got?

    Sam puts the box down.

Sam Fucking look, will you?

    Tom looks in.

Make you forget your troubles, eh?

Tom Jesus. They dead?

Sam Naaa.

Tom Can I touch?

Sam What you asking me for?

    Tom puts his hand into the box. Takes out a kitten.

Tom Where'd'you find them. Sweetheart. The blue eyes he's got.

Sam She. (*Sam's got the other one.*)

Tom How d'you know.

Sam Boy wouldn't look at you like that.

Tom Go on.

Sam Tortoiseshell. Don't get boy ones.

Tom Look at her, then. Fucking sweetheart. (*He's cradling the kitten.*) What they doin' here?

Sam Left them to die.

226

Pause.

Tom What kinda bastard's it take to kill a thing like this? I'll have their balls. I will. Little beauty. Listen to her. Listen.

Sam Tell her she's beautiful. Tell her and tell her. It's all she wants. You tell her that and she'll eat out your hand.

Tom Left you out to die. Did they? Did they? You're safe now. I've got you. I've got you. What's the person like, that could leave you to die? Bet their mammy's greeting for them. Lost yer mammy. Poor wee girl. Mewing now. Listen. Wee voice on it. Listen. Need feedin' Sam. What're we gonnie do.

Sam My Mum'll take them.

Tom Come on then.

Sam Not yet.

Tom Eh?

Sam We're supposed to be at school, remember. She's great my mum. Some things though. Some things she won't tolerate. 'Jeopardising your future.' 'Present pleasure, future grief.' 'Boredom gives birth to creativity.' She's a great one for that. 'Only stupid people are bored.' School. I've not had a day off school. I've had pneumonia, I've been at school. God's my witness. I went to the school with my antibiotics clutched tight in my hand, a pat on the backside, and 'Pull yourself together'; that's what followed me down from the doorstep. 'Positive thinking.' 'You'll not end up like your father.' My father's a very clever man. My father's a list of initials after his name even he's forgotten the meaning of some of them. It's not my father's fault. She'll not believe the buses my mum. She'll give me the look. You know the look. They all do it. You're my beloved son and you've wounded me to the heart. It comes with the kit. The disappointment that you are to me. That look's a killer. 'After all my sacrifice.' 'I didn't ask to be born.' That's what she drive you to. 'I didn't ask to be born.' Then she tells you. Every pain of her labour she gives you. And the stitches they sewed her up with. She makes you feel them every one. ' "Ask", you're right you didn't "ask" to be born. "Ask"? You demanded.' She'll say we should have walked. 'Doesn't matter what other people do. You do the right thing. I'm not interested in other people.' I can't go home till school's well over and I've had the time to leg it back.

Tom's putting stuff on the fire.

Tom My mum won't have another animal in the house. Cats give her the willies she says. Bloody fleas she says. Mess the last one was after the fox. Didn't die right away. Got maggots in it before it died. I'm having this one. I'm having it. There's no one gonnie take this cat away from me. Jesus, Sam.

Sam What?

Tom She's licking me.

Sam Giving you a wash.

Tom Scratches. Rough tongue she's got. Think she likes me?

Sam She'd have to be fond to lick you. I wouldn't lick you. Thinks you're her mammy. Thinks you need a clean. Bloody right she is too. You niff, Tom O'Halloran, d'you know that?

Tom The nose on it. Whiskers. Jesus God, Sam, this wee girl's got curly whiskers.

Sam Been to the hairdressers.

Tom Had a perm. Fanny.

Sam Eh?

Tom Her name. Fanny.

Sam Fanny?

Tom What's wrong?

Sam Callin' a cat Fanny. Shoutin' for her down the street.

Tom What's wrong with that?

Sam You dumb or what are you? Fanny?

Tom I like it.

Sam Fanny?

Tom slips the kitten down inside his shirt.

Tom Sleep wee girl. Sleep. (*He's rocking to and fro.*)
Shhhhh. Shhhh. Shhh.

Sam Be singing it a bloody lullaby next. Folk should have
a kitten delivered every three months with the milk. (*He's
looking at his own. Slips it down inside his shirt. Laughs.*)
Jesus. Bloody tickles. 'Deliver them with the milk. Make
the world a better place.'

Tom Dying on the beach. Jesus Sam, Jesus. Fucking life.
You get born. Pushed out of the house soon as look at
you. Playschool. Nursery. Learn this. Learn that. What the
fuck for, eh? They're working. You're working. School
nine till four. Books. They're not bloody working and
that's bloody worse. I don't see them happy. Never see
them happy. Seen them laughing, seen that. Seen my mum
rolling on the floor laughing. Rolling around she was.
Frightened me to bloody death. Sod bloody books. I
bloody hate them. I'd rather bloody live. I'm in despair.
Let me bloody live. Forty minutes for lunch. Bloody
homework. Bloody clarinet. College. University. Work.
Work. What they fucking have kids for? Never fucking see

them. 'Bloody school holidays. I hate the school holidays.' You hear them say it. Right in front of you. No bloody shame. 'Under my feet. What am I supposed to do with you? I've my work.' Fuck it. Two wee kittens. What's it take to look after two wee kittens?

Sam I'm gonnie be a vet. Work in a park in Africa.

Tom Fucking park. Fucking park. That's not real. I'm gonnie pack the shelves in fucking Gateway.

Sam You are not.

Tom That's where I'm heading. That's what Crockett told me. Told my mum. 'I'm disappointed in you.' That's what she said. Hired a fucking Maths tutor. Gave him a fucking door key. Key to my house. I get in, he's waitin' for me. Mother's not there. House is cold. There's a Maths tutor waiting for me. School nine to four. Tutor five to six. Homework seven to nine. Bed. Nine to four. Five to six. Seven to nine. Bed. Get up. Fucking clarinet. 'Are you gonnie blow that thing or are you just gonnie stand there?' 'Reed's not wet.' 'Don't you give me that,' she says. They're in a concert, she says. Sailing off into Mozart's A. D'you think they stop, do you? D'you think they stop? Excuse me a minute, they say, do they? I'm afraid you'll have to wait. My reed's not wet. 'You must think I'm awful stupid.' I can't stand it when they practise their wit. Verbal bombs she's dropping on me. I've my hands over my head, I'm ducked down taking shelter. I have to pop my head out to laugh at her jokes. 'Research shows. Most folk what they regret. Are you listening to me. That they didn't stick to their music. That's what they regret. You'll stick to yours. I'll see you will. One day you'll thank me.' What do they want, eh? What do they fucking want? Fucking torture and you have to thank her for it. And if you don't she fucking cries. I don't know. I don't know. I don't know.

Pause.

Sam You're not gonnie pack the shelves in Gateway.

Tom No harm in that. Eh sweetheart? No harm at all.

Sam wanders down the beach. Picks up a stone and flings it out on the ice. Bends holding the kitten under his shirt at his waist. Searches out flat stones. Gathers as many as he can find.

The sun gleams in through the hall window. Nita brings a china bowl down the stairs. Steam rising from it. And a cloth folded over its side.

Nita I found this in your mother's bedroom. I hope you don't mind. It's beautiful. She's got taste, your mother. Thinking to buy this.

Alex What are you doing?

Nita Sit still. (*She kneels by him.*) I fancied you. (*She touches his foot.*)

Alex Hey.

Nita What?

Alex Tickles.

Nita I've been at that bus stop every day. Weeks I've been there for. (*She wrings the cloth out in the water. Holds the hot cloth on his foot.*) Nice?

Alex Uh huh.

Nita To see you go past. You really didn't see me? Never seen me?

Alex No.

Nita Really?

Alex I didn't see you. I . . .

Nita What?

Alex I wish I had.

She pulls the cloth between his toes.

Nita Always wash between your toes. Touch me. (*She turns to him.*) Touch me.

But he doesn't.

Will I wash the other foot?

Alex I'd like that.

Nita Water's not too hot?

Alex It's fine.

Nita I'll get a towel. I'm sorry, I forgot the towel.

Alex cups her cheek in his hand. Alex kisses her.

Elspeth Budge up a bit.

Tom leaps to his feet.

Tom I beg your pardon.

Elspeth Nice fire.

Tom Yes.

Elspeth Can I share it with you?

Tom Please.

Elspeth I could do with a warm.

Tom I'd be delighted.

Elspeth Is that right? (*She sits.*) Good way to get piles this.

Tom I'm sorry?

Elspeth Sitting on cold stone. Don't let me keep you from the warm. (*She pats the stone beside her.*)

Tom Thank you.

Elspeth I've treacle toffees, would you like one.

She holds out a hand with three treacle toffees in it. He crouches down by her. Takes a toffee.

Tom You're very kind.

Elspeth One for your friend. He was the singer, was he?

Tom Voice like a corncrake me.

Elspeth Nothing like a boy's voice. I always liked a boy's voice best. Boys. I should have had a son. (*She puts out her hand and touches Tom's cheek.*) Girls are hard. Hard to rear. Hard of heart. A boy now, a boy, you can do something with a boy. I bet . . . Is that a good toffee?

His teeth are sticking together.

Tom Very nice, thank you.

Elspeth I bet you've got a lot of girlfriends.

Pause.

Tom Some.

Elspeth Have they names?

Pause.

Tom Tanya.

Elspeth Yes.

Tom She's the one I fancy. Katie wears Fila.

Elspeth Fila?

Tom Can't stand girls in Fila shoes. You know suede

trainers. Boot things. Black. Worse than Champion, Fila. Caterpillar I like. Caterpillar are cool. Doc Martens. I love a girl in Doc Martens. Laces all undone. Doccers make a girl look delicate. Snap their ankles with your fingers. Even girls with big calves they look good in Doccers. Eight holes. I don't like them higher than eight. Yellow stitching.

Elspeth That what Tanya wears?

Tom Bare feet. Winter even. Stones even. She's got this dress. Like a gypsy thing. Black. And it's got badges on. She looks . . .

Pause.

Elspeth And she's your girlfriend.

Tom No chance. She'll never ask me out. Knows I like her. Everyone knows I like her.

Elspeth Why don't you ask her?

Tom Doesn't go like that.

Elspeth Try.

Tom She's fourteen. Things they expect of you at fourteen. I can't . . . Her friends all say she likes me. Jesus. I like talking to her. She's a good talker. I'd run if she asked me out. I'd run a mile. Scared shitless I'd be. (*Shrugs.*) I beg your pardon.

Sam's throwing stones. Skiffing them across the ice. Muttering. Counting the skiffs. Throws.

Sam One two. (*Throws.*) One two three. (*Throws.*) One. Shit. (*Throws.*) One two three four.

Flashlight.

Frances Do you mind if I . . .

Elspeth and Tom turn to her.

Don't look. Go on talking. They way you were. You had your hand up . . .

Two frozen faces looking at her.

Tom You take snaps for a living.

Frances Pictures.

Tom You like it?

Elspeth The boy's asking you a question.

Frances On a good day.

Tom Why?

Frances Why?

Elspeth Why?

Frances I'm not telling you. I don't trust you.

Elspeth Would you say that to your mother. Would you?

Tom What do you see?

Elspeth What can she see, for God's sake? That's a shield she's holding up in front of her.

Frances I see you very clearly.

Elspeth Weddings, Frances, that's where you're headed.

Frances This sees what I tell it. Often and often, it'll sniff out more. It'll see the person if they'll let it. If I'm lucky, it'll sense their secrets, too, and lay them out every single one.

Tom (*Takes out kitten. He digs the kitten out from inside his shirt.*) Look, didn't see her, did it?

Elspeth Chaos, my lass. You have to open out your arms and let chaos in. Don't you smile like that. You know all about chaos and I know you do. I've seen your bedroom.

Frances hoots with laughter. Tom joins in.

Why's that funny? Go on, laugh, I don't care.

Tom See the grey she's got under her eyes. Does her eyes the same as you.

Frances So she does.

Tom I like your eyes.

Frances Thank you.

Tom I like your hair.

Frances You're very kind.

Tom Can I have a touch?

Elspeth Will I leave you two alone?

Tom Can I touch your hair?

Frances Feel free.

He rubs the hair at the back of her head.

Tom Bristly.

Frances Is it?

Tom Tickles.

Frances Does it?

Tom Nice that. Really nice.

Frances Are you done?

Tom Thanks.

Frances Ready?

Tom Don't you flash that camera though. She's a baby. Only just opened her eyes. Don't you hurt her eyes.

Frances takes the pictures of Tom and the kitten. Talks

through the clicking and whirring.

Frances Beautiful eyes.

Tom Left on the beach she was.

Frances Little thing.

Tom Left her to die.

Elspeth Bloody *Sun* readers.

Frances You don't know that.

Elspeth Frances, I know it. I know it like I saw them do it.

Tom Makes you sad this weather. Makes me sad anyway.

The camera whirring on through her mother's anger.

Elspeth *Sun* readers. They're the ones. And you'd know it, too, but you're so damn liberal you don't know what you know. Your instincts are so squashed. So perverted . . . You've forgotten how to be honest. That's what's wrong with your photographs. *Sun* readers, I'm telling you.

The camera's at rest.

Tom That it? That us done?

Frances Thank you.

Tom Had enough of us Lamb. You and me. Done us now. Moving on.

Elspeth Little baby. Little darling. (*She listens to the kitten.*) She's hungry.

She fishes in her pocket. The cigarette falls out. And some toffees. She doesn't notice. Tom does. He shuffles to hide them.

Here. You take this.

Tom I couldn't possibly . . .

Elspeth Buy that baby some milk.

Tom tucks the kitten away. Takes the money. Palms the cigarettes. Pockets them.

Tom Dropped your toffees. (*Hands over the sweets.*)

Sam Six seven eight nine. Yeeeeeeees. (*Yelling back to Tom.*) Niner, niner.

Elspeth Off you go to your friend. Off you go. Off you go. Don't mind me. You have fun with your friend. Tell him I liked his voice. Tell him . . . (*Pokes at the fire with a stick, makes it flame. Holds a hand out to it.*) See through my hands. The blood running through my hands. That's time and I'm watching it. Running and running. Belting away from me. Time to cut my hair and have a boy touch it. I never had a boy touch my hair. A man touching me. Too many years. Too, too many. And all of them gone.

Tom's climbing down the rocks to Sam. Sam throws again.

Sam Two three four.

And again, Tom's getting closer.

Two three. Fuck. (*And again.*) Two three four five six. Sevener. Sevener.

Tom Sixer.

Sam See that, did you? Rises on the bumps. Rises on the waves where they're frozen. Bloody perfection. Perfection I'm telling you. (*A couple of slow motion practice goes. Taking the arm back. Leaning into it.*) Just turned. Just skiffed. The beauty of it. This bloke in America. Twenty he can get. On water mind. Fucking twenty. Spends all day at it. Twenty-five sometimes. All day just skiffing. That's his whole life. The perfect stone. The perfect throw.

Tom My mum was school champion at the shotput. (*Tom*

picks up a heavy stone and puts it.) Eeeeeeasy.

    Sam picks one up and puts it further than Tom.

Sam Yes.

    Then Tom.

Tom Fuck.

    Then Sam.

Sam Yes, yes, yes.

    Tom gets a cigarette between his teeth.

Tom Light?

Sam Where'd you get those?

Tom I let an old lady touch me up. Want one?

Sam Naaaa! (*He lights Tom's. Lets the match burn to the bottom. Blows it out. Shrugs and wipes his hands.*)

Tom It's hard that ice.

    Pause.

We could go out on it.

Sam Haar's coming in.

Tom All the better. Go for a walk on the ice.

Sam What for?

Tom See how far we could get.

Sam Could break.

Tom Fucking stone thumping down on it, that didn't break it.

    Silence.

Did it?

Sam No.

Tom Well then?

Sam Haar could cut us off.

Tom You're feart.

Sam I'm not.

Tom Aye you are.

Sam Aye I'm not.

Tom I'm going if you're not.

Sam I'm not stopping you.

Tom I'll go on my own.

Sam Go on.

Tom Right then.

Sam Right.

Tom You comin'?

Sam No.

Tom Fuck off then.

Sam Fuck off yourself.

  Tom steps out. Sam watches.

Tom We'll go, won't we, Fanny? You and me. (*He gets further out. He shouts back*.) Safe as fucking houses.

Sam Watch that kitten.

Tom She's got a fucking name.

Sam Watch her though.

Tom She's alright.

Sam Fucking watch her, that's all.

Tom She's alright with me. I'll see no harm comes to you. Sweatheart. Eh? Sweetheart. You and me.

Sam Tom. Get lost in the haar. Tom. Tom.

Tom shouts back.

Tom Fucking magic out here. No one else in all the world, Fanny. You and me. Just you and me. (*Gradually he's isolated.*) And a warm fire waiting on the beach for when we go back. If we go back. We could walk to another land from here. See it, Fanny. A far-off land. My mum keeps escape money. The Caribbean, she says. Ever since she had her first job. 'It's there,' she says. 'If I need it. And none of you ask me for it. Don't care what it's for. If you lose a leg and you need my money for a new one you'll not get it.' She was wicked my mum. Put wasps in the swiss rolls. Wish I'd known her when she was wicked. We're ice people you and me and this is our land.

Sam Tooooooooom.

Sam's yelling from the shore. Tom yells back. They can't see each other.

Tom Wanker. Turn your back on the shore, Fanny. Don't look round. That's the trick. This is a fresh land our land. End of that old world. No one's been here ever before. That's a fucking miracle. Eh? See the rock. We'll get past that. We will so. Then there'll be nothing. Just nothing. And all the time in the world for it.

Sam I'm coming. Wait for me. I'm coming.

Tom Put your paws over your ears. Had his chance. Had his bloody chance. (*Tom tramps on.*)

Sam Waaaaaa-ii-t.

A blaze of sunlight on Tom. Then shade.

Alex Here. Come here. Come on. Nita.

Nita What. (*Opens up the window. Cracks off an icicle.*)

Alex Drips icicles. It's a thaw. Feel the damp in the air. Want one? Ice-pole.

Nita Shut the window. Shut the bloody window.

The window slams down. Nita sits on the stairs, Alex massages her shoulders.

The sun shines on Sam. He takes his blazer off. Takes his jumper off. Puts his blazer on. Fishes the kitten out from inside his shirt. Wraps the kitten in the jumper. Puts it in the box.

Sam You stay here. Stay in the warm. I'll be back. Wait for me. You hear me. No going off with any other fucker that takes your fancy. I'll be back for you. And we'll have some milk, eh? In my mum's warm kitchen. And the windows all steamed up. We'll have some milk you and me.

The light follows him out on to the ice.

Alex has his hand at Nita's neck, gripping.

Nita You're hurting me.

Alex Shit.

Nita What is it? Alex?

Then he lets her go. Bounds down the stairs turning all the photographs to face the wall. Alex picks up two frames and runs downstairs. Drops one. The glass shatters.

Alex Mind out. Mind your feet.

Nita Oh Jesus.

Her foot's cut before she can avoid the glass. Alex swings her up into his arms.

I'm sorry.

Alex You're dripping blood. (*Puts her in front of the fire.*) Are you alright? (*Grabs the damp cloth and holds it to her foot.*)

Sam Tooooooom. Tooooooom. Tooooooom. Clouds coming in. Dark swooping in. Jesus. Jesus it's thin there. (*He picks up a piece of ice.*) How's it get broken, eh? How's it bloody broken. There's not a soul been out here. Jesus no. Tom. Tom, you wanker. Fucking come here.

There's a creaking as he's standing there.

Tooooooom. I'm cold to my bones. (*Chucks the ice so that it slithers a long, long way. The noise of its passage echoes.*) Come here, wanker.

Alex is sweeping up the glass with a dustpan and brush. Nita wrings out the cloth and holds it to her foot. She shudders. He comes over puts more wood on the fire.

Nita Make it colder.

Alex Flare up in a minute.

Nita Bowl's full of blood.

He picks it up.

Alex I'll get fresh water.

Nita Alex?

Alex What is it?

Nita Turn the pictures round.

He shakes his head.

Turn them round, Alex, please.

Alex They creak these houses. They're haunted. 'Sakes alive Miss Scarlett, I's scared of hants.'

Nita They're not haunted.

Alex Hear it. Listen.

Pause.

My dad haunts this one.

Nita Stop it.

Alex There. There, there he goes.

Nita What?

Alex Missed him.

Nita Stop it.

Alex Three days before my dad died there was a dove on the roof. Shh. (*He grabs hold of her shoulders. Twists her round.*) Look, look.

She twists out of his grasp. Belts him full across the face. They're facing each other. Kneeling there in front of the fire.

Beautiful bird it was. Got the ladder out. My mum went up the ladder. Gets her hands to the bird. My dad's at the window. He's hauled himself out of the bed. 'Leave it,' my dad says. Bird wasn't hurt. We left it. My dad goes into a coma. His breathing filled this house. Waiting for each breath. Me and my mum and the bird. Willing him to breathe. Breathing for him. Willing him not to breathe. Not to. He's in a coma for three days. He dies. The bird flies off. Waiting for him, see. (*Teasing*.) See that door there. Up there. See it. See it's open.

Nita What about it?

Alex Try and shut it. Go on.

Nita Why?

Alex Hasn't shut since my dad died. We've had a carpenter in to that door. Know what it is.

Nita What?

Alex He's hanging about. I've seen more of my dad round this place since he died than I did when he was alive. It's my Mum. 'Frances'. 'Frances'. He wants her. He's waiting for her. 'Frances'. A love like theirs. Her nursing him. Doing it all for him. Used to stand up by that mirror there. And her with him. Just look at himself. Flesh melting off him. Her holding him. Arm at his back there. Hand on his arm. The two of them. (*He yells up to where the mirror is.*) Can you not eat? Fucking eat something. Bloody starving to death. Too much skin on his body. Skin moving over the bones. Holding him and holding him. Till his body hurt him, so she couldn't hold him any more. Held him then with her eyes. (*And in anger.*) Leaving me to look after her. She was sleek my mum when he was alive. Skin of silk. He kept her sleek. He wants her now. Go on up and try that door. Go on. Maybe he'll let you shut it. (*She kneels there looking at him. He rubs his cheek.*) You've a hard hand. My gran gets through to her. Habit. My gran puts bait on her hook and my mother rises to it.

Elspeth grabs a flare from the fire. Gets to her feet. It's dark on the beach. Cloudy evening darkness.

Elspeth Where's my damn cigarettes? Where are they? (*She's shining it round.*) Have you got them?

Frances What would I want with them?

Elspeth What would I want with them?

Frances Mother!

Elspeth Mother!

   Pause.

Och well.

Frances I haven't got your cigarettes.

Elspeth Where are they then?

Frances I don't know.

   Pause.

Elspeth Fire's dying.

   They both watch the fire.

Frances Come on Mother. I'm chilly.

Elspeth I like a fire.

Frances Take me in.

Elspeth Where are those boys?

Frances Off on their adventures.

Elspeth Can't leave this burning.

   Frances kicks it out.

That's a sad sight. He liked your hair. Can I feel it?

   *Frances bends. Her mother rubs her hand over the
   prickly hair at the nape of her neck. Elspeth laughs.*

Tickles right enough. Are you having a good day, cherub? I
am. A rare day. (*Puts her hands deep in her pocket.*) They
were nice boys, good boys. Think he took my cigarettes?

Frances Come on in.

Elspeth I don't care if he did. Let him. If it gives him pleasure. Have you any in the house?

Frances I don't smoke.

Elspeth I didn't ask you that. I asked you if you had any cigarettes.

Frances Yes.

Elspeth Have you?

Frances Yes, yes. I've got some, I've got cigarettes.

Elspeth I'm not deaf, Frances.

Frances Come and I'll give you a cigarette and I'll smoke one with you if it'll make you happy.

Elspeth Are you going to Australia, Frances? Are you going to live there?

Frances It's a beautiful land.

Elspeth You'd miss me in Australia.

Frances Maybe I would.

Elspeth You'd miss me, Frances.

Frances Like a hole in the head.

Elspeth Don't go to Australia.

   The ice moves. Splits.

Frances Mist coming in. (*She holds her arm out to her mother.*)

Elspeth I don't need your arm. I'll manage fine without it.

Frances Take my bloody arm, Mother. (*She holds it out. Pause.*)

Elspeth My name's Elspeth.

Frances Take my arm, Elspeth, please.

Elspeth takes it.

Elspeth A nice walk round by the lighthouse. Warm us up. (*Her hand is vague in the air. Frances holds it.*) Maybe I'll make a table that I can leave behind me. A good strong table with legs that I'd turned on a lathe.

Frances laughs.

Work that you can see. And when you leave it. There it is. Solid. Bearing witness. Don't you go away to some hot land. That's no answer, Frances. These photographs. These that you took today, these are good photographs. I'm telling you.

The light from the lighthouse makes its slow journey across the ice. It catches Sam. Moves on. Catches him again.

Sam Tom, come on, you wanker. Got to take that kitten home. Got to get it out the cold. Hungry wee thing. Tooooom. Tooooom.

Sam walks on. Ice splintering around him. Nita runs up the stairs to the telescope. Alex after her. Sam's bending down on the ice.

No. No. Jesus. (*Crouching down, scooping Fanny into his arms.*) Jesus, Fanny, where is he? He's no gone through. Has he gone through? And I canny see. I canny see a bloody thing. (*He holds the kitten away from him.*) Jesus. Help me.

Chloe's caught in the light. She stumbles.

Chloe Oh my God. Lily. Lily! (*Chloe, eyes closed, head up, grips on to the prom rail.*)

Lily Are you alright?

Chloe Is that you?

Lily For goodness sake, who do you think it is. Open your eyes, Chloe. For God's sake, what's wrong with you.

Chloe I fell.

Lily You did no such thing.

Chloe I fell. I fell.

Lily You hold on any tighter to that rail, the bones'll come through your skin. Hold on any tighter they'll come bursting through. Then you'll be sorry, you'll be sorry alright. You should have gloves, Chloe. Iron can burn. Cold iron. Take the skin off your hands. Where's your damn gloves for God sake, Chloe. Coming out without gloves. At your age. I've given you gloves. Christmas and birthday you've had gloves from me. Sheepskin. Lined. Let go the rail. Let go, do you hear me? Holding on there. Making a spectacle of yourself.

Chloe Who's to see?

Lily You're speaking, are you?

Chloe Don't be stupid.

Lily I thought you'd lost your tongue. Let go that rail and come on home with me.

Chloe No.

Lily Houses have windows, Chloe. You're in public.

Chloe Am I the one that's shouting? Am I? Shouting and waving my arms about? That they should be looking at me. Am I?

Lily Don't you speak to me like that.

Chloe You show me who's looking at me.

Lily Tone of voice.

Chloe In this God-forsaken and desolate place there isn't a soul alive that's looking at me.

Lily The dark's coming in.

Chloe I'm standing here, that's all I'm doing. What harm is there in that? You tell me.

Lily You'll freeze to that rail.

Chloe What harm is there?

Lily I don't know what's wrong with you.

Chloe I fell.

Lily It's treacherous. You slipped, that's all.

Chloe I let go of this. Take a finger off this. I let go. I'll fall again.

Lily Don't be . . .

Chloe I'll fall . . .

Lily You will not.

Chloe I'm telling you.

Lily Oh for God's sake.

Chloe That ground's waiting for me.

Pause.

Lily Take my arm.

Chloe Bring us both down.

Lily I'm strong. Take my arm.

Pause.

Do you think I can't hold you? Eh? Do you? I can hold
you.

Chloe I never slipped.

Lily We've a funeral to go to on Thursday.

Chloe I lost the world. As God's my witness. The world
went away from me. I didn't slip. The world fell away.

Lily It's been a long day.

Chloe You took your time getting to me, Lily. It was all
black. Thick black. Didn't know where I was. Don't know
where I am yet.

Lily I've two pair of Arbroath Smokies. All packeted up
nice with their bit butter. I was saving them. We'll pop
them in the pan, Chloe. A bit toast. Take my arm now. I'll
not let you fall.

Chloe Kippers?

Lily Arbroath Smokies.

Chloe I don't like kippers.

Lily Arbroath Smokies, Chloe. For God's sake are you
deaf?

Chloe He said we were all dragonflies. That man. When
we were alive we were larva in the mud.

Lily Larvae.

Chloe When we died we spread our iridescent wings in the
sunshine of God's love and frolicked. That minister. With
the drip at his nose. That's what he said. That minister.

Lily You take my arm.

Chloe What the hell did he mean?

Lily It was a metaphor.

Chloe A metaphor?

Lily Nothing wrong with a dragonfly.

Chloe Are we maggots in the slime, Lily? Is that all we are?

Lily Didn't know what he was talking about. Did he? Did he? Take my arm, Chloe. You'll not fall. You see, I'll make sure you don't fall. Look at the light all fading. (*She holds out her arm.*) That ice is cracking. The fog there'll be this night. There'll be a thaw. The waves'll run tomorrow. They'll run alright. I'm telling you, you won't fall.

   Chloe puts her hand on Lily's arm.

That man had holes in his cassock, Chloe. The minister. He was overweight and his chest was none too good. Maybe he likes dragonflies, poor old soul. In the middle of winter, Christmas gone, the very dearth of the year. Dragonflies in the sun.

Chloe I don't want to be a bloody dragonfly when I die, Lily. They live for a day dragonflies. That's all they have in the sunlight. I don't want my heaven to be a single day of bliss and then oblivion. I want more.

Lily Bliss? Dragging him out of his bed. The odd funeral. Maybe it keeps him in pipe tobacco, eh? Poor old soul. Maybe he was a fisherman, eh? With his dragonflies. That's right. That's my good girl. Step by step. We've letters to write you and me. After all we saw her a week ago. Thursday's funeral. We were practically in at the death. That's a thrill, eh, Chloe? You'll not fall while I'm here. After all what harm do they do? Eh? Dragonflies? No harm. No harm at all.

   They cross each other: Chloe and Lily; Frances and Elspeth.

Nita Your mother's coming back.

Alex Will I see you again?

Nita Maybe.

Alex Will I though?

Nita I'll be at the bus stop.

Alex I mean see you.

Nita I know what you mean.

Alex Will I then?

Nita Probably.

Elspeth Listen. It's a boy playing that.

Frances Is it?

The clarinet is louder.

Sam's kneeling on the ice. The light swirls over him.

Sam Tooooooom.

Frances What's that?

Elspeth Boys. Tttt. Tttt. Tttt. Tttt.

Frances Are they alright?

Elspeth What could happen to them? Shhhh.

Frances What?

Elspeth Did you hear a kitten?

Frances No.

And they're gone. The light fades. ·

Sam Toooooooom. Toooooooom.

'Piano' very loud. The light fades to blackout.

BORDERS OF PARADISE

For Cal, Chris, Jonathan, Benny, Guy, Joe,
Tom, Barry, Sat, Will, Morgan and Keira.

Characters

Rob
David
Rose
Ellen
Charlie
Cot
John

Five English boys and two Scottish girls
on a North Devon beach.

This version of **Borders of Paradise** was first performed at Watford Palace on 16 March 1995. The cast was as follows:

Rob Tat Whalley
David Mark Letheren
Rose Pauline Turner
Ellen Kathy Kiera Clarke
Charlie Karl Collins
Cot Paul Sharma
John Tom Wisdom

Directed by Lou Stein
Designed by Emma Donovan
Music by Identity Crisis
Lighting by Richard Johnson

Act One

Torchlight. Sound of surf.

Rob Cold?

David Na. You?

Rob Na.

   They are, though.

David Rob?

Rob W-what?

David See it?

Rob I see it.

David See it? Jesus.

Rob We're here.

David Rob.

Rob We're here.

David Yeeeeeeees.

   Running. Torches waving.

Jeeeeeeesus.

Guitar. A match flares on a height. A hand lights a hurricane lamp. Flaring shadows on canvas. **Ellen** *and* **Rose** *are inside a small tent high up on a cliff, against a dark, very early morning sky.*

Rose What the fuck're you doing?

Ellen Quiet.

Rose Ellen?

Ellen There's someone there.

Rose There is not.

Ellen Listen.

  A moment.

Rose Waves, Ellen.

Ellen Chuckies moving.

Rose Pebbles falling down the cliff.

Ellen The cliff's falling on us.

Rose Only slightly.

Ellen The cliff's falling on us. Is that what you're telling me?

Rose Relax.

Ellen For fuck sake how can I relax?

Rose Go back to sleep Ellen.

Ellen And wake up dead?

  A trickle of stones.

Oh God.

Rose What if it's him?

Ellen Better him than the fucking cliff yes?

Rose Shit, shit, shit.

Ellen He's not going to kill us, is he?

Rose You tell anyone we were coming here?

Ellen No.

Rose You did, you told.

Ellen I did not. Don't you fucking trust me?

Rose Can't be him then, can it?

Ellen My mother I told.

Rose Oh God, Ellen.

Ellen I had to.

Rose I'm running away for Christ sake.

Ellen I'm not.

Rose As well shout it from the fucking rooftops as tell your mother.

Ellen I want her to know where I am.

Rose What for?

Ellen In case, alright, case the cliff falls on my head so she'll know where to find my dead body. I like to think of her cradling me, that would comfort me while I'm suffocating. Christ, Rose. I like my Mother.

Rose I'll die if he's followed us.

Ellen Don't die here. I'm not hauling your dead body up this cliff.

A moment.

Got a knife?

Rose What for?

Ellen Case he rips open the canvas and bursts in here.

Rose What's he going to do that for?

Ellen Make women of us. What else?

Rose He's a fucking English teacher. He's not fucking Sean Penn.

Ellen English teachers have got dicks, Rose.

Rose Peaceful dicks.

Ellen That's an oxymoron isn't it ?

Rose He's not here. He's at home with his wife. Curled up in bed where he belongs.

Ellen You wish.

Rose I can't hear a thing. (*Rose listens.*) It's you.

Ellen What?

Rose You're breathing too hard.

Ellen I've got a blocked-up nose.

Rose Hold your breath. (*She listens.*) I can hear the wind. Waves I can hear. Nice safe wind. That's all.

Rose lies down. Ellen goes to blow out the light.

Leave it on.

Ellen I can't sleep with the light on.

Rose Please, Ellen.

Ellen turns it down.

Ellen That do you?

Rose Thank you.

Ellen I hate compromise. A woman should never compromise. You're the only one I'd compromise for.

Rose I'm very grateful.

Ellen Never for a man. Never, never, never.

Guitar. Torchlight. Behind the voices, sound of good surf.
Sets and a lull.

David What's that? Shit.

Rob What?

David Listen.

Rob For fuck's sake, D-Davey.

They're shifting the stuff the two of them. Picnic coolers,
boards, wet suits.

David Click. Hear it?

Rob Hear the sea D-Davey.

David Light switch. Bedclothes going back.

Rob What're you chatting about?

David My father.

Rob He's at home, Davey,

David Hear him from here. Pre-dawn run. Slap of his feet
on the cork floor. He's in the kitchen. I can hear the cotton
of his pyjamas brush as he walks. Crossing to the sink. I
know every move. I'm here. I can see it. Picking up the pill
bottle. Hand clenching round the top. Slight whistling of
his breath through his teeth. Click of the child lock. Hear
it? Click, click, click?

Rob I don't hear it.

David Click, see?

Rob I don't fucking hear it.

David Pill in his hand. Thank God, just one. Hand to
mouth. Jerks his head back. Pill lying against the tongue.
Tongue arched to take it. Turning the tap. Gush of water
in a glass. I hear him swallow. I could stand it if he was

physically ill. If his pain was tangible I could hold his hand. My tendons snap to the tune of that bottle. I'm here. I'm in front of this ocean. It is my place on this earth and I'm telling you I can hear the whirr of that bottle top. I can feel the grooves cut into my hand. My whole body's tense till it hurts. Feel my glands.

Rob Fuck off.

David My glands are swollen. I'm stressed out. Feel them.

Rob I d-don't want to feel your g-g-glands.

David I'd feel *your* glands.

Rob W-winds off the land. Make them stand up. They'll be walls. They'll be glassy. P-pisses me off when you c-come all this w-way and all you get's slop. Not today though. Today's p-perfect.

Guitar. In the tent on the height.

Ellen What if it's fellas?

Rose Don't think I could bear it.

Ellen Might be fun.

Rose Fellas have never been fun.

Ellen I live in hope.

Rose More fool you.

Ellen Don't start.

Rose Woman in the corner shop never called you sonny.

Ellen You don't look like a boy, Rose.

Rose Why'd she call me sonny then?

Ellen She's blind.

Rose In the pub. Come on Ellen, you were there. Man behind the bar refused to serve me.

Ellen Refused to serve me, too.

Rose 'What age are we tonight then, son?'

Ellen He was pissed.

Rose I had a skirt on.

Ellen Proves he was pissed.

Rose Don't let it be fellas. I don't want fellas.

Ellen This is a joke, right? For God sake, Rose. You're beautiful. Shit. You've got a man that's obsessed with you. That follows you everywhere and you're going nuts thinking you're a boy.

Rose He's gay's what I think.

Ellen He's married.

Rose In the mortuary, my mum. You get a lot of them in there dressed in women's clothes. Dead men. Beautiful clothes she says, and it's their wives that come to identify them.

Ellen Shit, Rose. Shit.

Rose She came home with this pair of shoes once. Nicked them off this fella. 'Bloody hell,' she says. 'Hardly bloody worn,' she says. 'If I had shoes like this I wouldn't commit suicide. He wants to try living off sausages three times a week, mozzarella on Fridays. This man has his own personal last,' she says, 'and he swallows cyanide. I even get my knickers from Oxfam. The label on these shoes,' she says. 'He doesn't deserve them. I deserve them.' So she nicks them.

Ellen I couldn't work in a mortuary.

Rose Bit like a delicatessen really. 'Gender isn't cut and dried,' she says. 'What is a woman after all?' That's what she says.

Ellen And what does she answer?

Rose shrugs.

Unless you were an immaculate conception she must know.

Rose 'Your Father might as well have been God,' she says. 'Number of times he's shown his face round here.'

Ellen Completely bloody intellectually flabby.

Rose Better than being physically flabby.

Ellen My mother has a problem with her glands.

Rose Your mother has a problem with the fish and chip shop down the road. Your mother could keep Mars bars going single-handed. She makes Jo Brand look like Twiggy.

Ellen 'Politics and principles died with the fall of the wall. There's only deep-fried pizzas left.' That's what she says. Says she's a sensationalist. I'm glad she's fat. She's nice to cuddle. She's always there. The thin ones are never there.

Rose See what I am. I'm an androgyne. That's why I suit him.

Ellen You're an idiot's what you are.

Rose Talks about my wrist bones, Ellen. My fucking wrist bones. Says he's never seen bones like I've got on my wrists. See if I show my wrist bones when he's around I feel like I'm giving him the come-on. I wear sleeves down to my knees. I don't want him. I don't want any man. I want you and me and the sun and the waves. I want to swim. I couldn't swim in front of fellas. I couldn't let them see me.

A voice singing. David's.

David

> 'The heart has narrow Banks
> It measures like the Sea.'

In simple thirds, Rob joins.

David

> 'In mighty – unremitting Bass
> And Blue monotony'

> 'To winter to remove
> with winter to abide
> Go manacle your Icicle
> against your Tropic Bride'

Ellen Emily fucking Dickinson for Christ sake. Jesus God. Hear that? Jesus, Rose.

Rose No, no, no, no, no.

Ellen Fellas. Fellas, Rose. (*She starts to crawl forward.*)

Rose What're you doing?

Ellen That's my future out there. I'm going to see what it looks like.

David

> 'Noon – is the hinge of the Day
> Evening – the tissue door –
> Morning – the East compelling the sill
> Till all the world is ajar.'

Rob Jesus. David. Look.

David What?

Rob You looking?

David What?

Rob Sun, see.

Ellen Look, look, look, look.

Rose My God. My God.

Rob Dawn.

David No, no. Shit. It can't come yet.

The light builds.

Shit.

Rob B-beauty of it.

David Where are they? Where the fuck are they?

Rob Quiet, D-Davey.

David The day had to start with the dawn.

Rob Starting then.

David All of us together and the dawn.

Rob Quiet.

Guitar. Light. The sound of gulls.

Rose You're in my light.

Ellen What?

Rose Get out of my light.

Ellen Excuse me.

Rose Right.

Ellen What are you doing, for God's sake?

Rose I'm bathing amn't I.

Ellen Am I missing something, Rose?

Rose It's a dawn, isn't it?

Ellen Is this some pagan rite I'm witnessing here?

Rose What if? I'm trying to concentrate.

Ellen You could be rolling in dog shit.

Rose Will you let me concentrate?

Ellen All this way for you to roll around. You could have done that at home.

The light builds.

David My father right? My father. He's having this nervous breakdown. See that's what his therapist says. Therapist says he's having this breakdown because me and my sister are getting older, see. Because we don't need him. Happens to a lot of men she says. I need him. I like him. He's sitting at the dinner table, my father. The meals he cooks. I love the meals he cooks. Like a sunset the food he cooks. Like a dawn. We've just had a five course meal/ we've had asparagus.

Rob I l-like *t-tiramisu*.

David In puff pastry and a hollandaise sauce, sabayon, you know.

Rob No.

David Doesn't fucking matter. We've had aubergine all flattened out to a purple pie shape and filled with its own self and tomatoes and peppers and thick but light, you know.

Rob No.

David Fucking telling you. He serves it on a platter and there's diamonds of tomato by it. Looks like a still life. We've had chestnuts and shallots in a red wine sauce that he's served with a *mousseline* of potatoes that's so light you don't know they're there. These potatoes. Froth on the tongue, man. The cheese course is little goat's cheese soufflés served with a salad of *radicchio* and corn leaves dressed in balsamic vinegar.

Rob I l-like chips with my vinegar.

David We've had summer pudding. And we've had a fudge chocolate thing that only he makes and he's decorated it with stars. And the whole thing's been perfection so he's pleased. And I'm happy for him. He's taking a holiday from his nervous breakdown. And then he starts. He starts on how he used to be a fan of this country but now he'd rather live in Italy. How the Italians are the people they are because they live amidst beauty. How the Americans have hope because they have vast horizons. They're not dull like us.

Cot, John and Charlie creep down the cliff.

We're the brick people. That's what he says. Bricks are the sum of our achievement. I like bricks. Yellow bricks. Red bricks. I like that they start at Carlisle and they mean England. But he's whanging on about Italy and style. And Americans and hope. And I say the Romans had bricks but he doesn't listen. 'Artists are Italian,' he says. 'There are no British artists. No British composers. Dreamers are American. There are no British dreamers. We are constricted by our impoverished landscape,' he says. Wish he was here now. See this. This is the landscape that made me. This is beauty.

The boys pounce on David and Rob.

John Yeees.

David Fuck off.

Rob Shit.

Charlie I've been starving since Taunton.

Cot You had a bacon roll and two doughnuts.

Charlie I'm a growing boy.

John See the waves out by Kate's Maw.

Charlie See them in close.

John Kate's Maw though.

Charlie You're not going out there.

John See them though.

Charlie You go out there. You go alone.

John Davey'll come.

Rob Girls. Girls here. In this place. My G-G-God.

> *Full sunlight*
> *John puts his hand on David's shoulder.*

You missed the fucking dawn.

John Sorry Davey.

David You missed it.

John Be another tomorrow.

David Be clouds tomorrow.

John You always say that. Be no surf, you say. Be clouds, you say.

David It was a perfect dawn and you missed it.

John Saw it from up there.

David Point was to see it together. All of us together.

Cot Was the same dawn.

Charlie Got lost, didn't we?

Cot His mother.

Charlie 'Turn right,' we say.

Cot 'What?' she says.

Charlie points with each hand.

Charlie 'That right or that right?' she says.

John 'Keep your hands on the wheel,' we say.

Cot 'I'm steering with my knees,' she says.

Charlie She turns left.

John She's wired up wrong. Gets worse when she's premenstrual. Doesn't get tense, my mother, just can't park the car. Only way she knows she's coming on, she says. Never been any good with dates. Didn't notice she was pregnant until she was five months gone. Then she felt this lump. 'Oh my God I'm dying,' she says to my father. 'Feel this.' 'That's a baby,' he says. She fainted. 'What's going to happen at menopause?' she says. 'Will I ever drive again?'

Charlie I fucking hope not.

Rose is gripping on to Ellen.

Rose Get back.

Ellen My heart's turning over, Rose.

Rose See you in your night things, they'll think it's a come-on.

Ellen Disappointed?

Rose What?

Ellen It's not your man followed you all the way here leaving his wife and children to be close to you.

Rose He's never been close to me.

Ellen That's how you keep him dangling.

Rose I've never encouraged him.

Ellen You've never told him no.

Rose It's not like that. You know it.

Ellen How do I?

Rose Don't you fight with me.

Ellen Maybe if you'd gone up to him and said stop following me. Maybe if you'd done that, been straight with him. He'd have stopped.

Rose Just have told me I was imagining things, wouldn't he?

Ellen Well, maybe you are. I'm bloody sick of it I tell you.

Rose I'm bloody sick of you.

Pause.

Ellen Who's making the beans then?

Rose I am.

Ellen Bloody make them then.

A moment.

Rose Ellen?

Ellen What?

Rose I've got binoculars. Want them?

Rose rummages in the tent.

Rose If he came up to me and said, 'Want a bonk?' I could say piss off. Doesn't though, does he? Looks is all. His looks, though, eat me up. The showers I take to wash his looks off me.

Ellen I know. I know.

Rose Says to me, 'When I was a boy I wanted to write an immortal book. When I was a youth I wanted to write an immortal poem. Now I am a man and know that immortality is only fashion, I would be grateful if I could write a meaningful line, speak a meaningful word.'

Ellen What did you say?

Rose Wanker.

Ellen You did not.

Rose Should have.

Ellen I think it's a sad and beautiful thing to say.

Rose The whole of English literature that he carries with him, looks out of his eyes at me. Every man that's fancied a woman. Every touch that's ever been written. Looking out of his eyes and touching me.

Pause.

Ellen Sounds wonderful.

Rose Ellen.

Ellen Could have a different lover every night. D. H. Lawrence, you could have, Chaucer, Shelley, Byron, Roger McGough. What teachers they'd be to tell you what a woman is.

Pause.
Rose examines herself.

What the fuck're you doing, Rose? Stop pulling yourself about.

Rose Thought maybe if I sat in a dawn, if I bathed in it I'd be different. I'm not Ellen. I'm not. I'm still me. I should've concentrated then I'd be different. I didn't concentrate that's what's wrong. Oh God, Ellen, you don't get a second chance with a dawn.

Ellen Make love in it, you'd be different then. Sun's shining Rose. Day's full of promise.

Rose What they like?

Ellen They're the lost boys.

Rose Stupid cow.

Ellen Perfect. Completely bloody gorgeous. Gorgeous, gorgeous, gorgeous. I'm wetting my knickers.

Sunlight on the viewing platform.

Charlie Yeeeeeeeeeeeeeeees.

Rob and Charlie charge down the steps to the beach whooping all the way, leaving **Cot** *and Davey on the cliff-top.*

Rob Surf's uuuuuuuuup.

John stops.

John You're going in, aren't you?

David Don't need me.

John You running out on me?

David What're we talking about?

John Guilty conscience, Davey?

David We talking about surfing?

John You're fucking us over.

David Shit, man.

John Driving along, thinking of surf. She lays this on me, my mother. Casually, yeah. Assumed I knew.

David They hear?

John Asleep. Better tell them, Davey. ' 'Fore I do.

David You surfing or what? Go on. Tide's right.

John Knew she'd tell me didn't you. Couldn't do it yourself.

David Mind Charlie doesn't break his neck.

John That the way you're playing it?

David Fucking perfect John. See it?

John Tell them Davey, yeah?

David Yeah. Right.

John goes on down. David looks at Cot.

What?

Cot You going?

David Maybe.

Cot Afraid?

David Want to go down?

Cot No hurry.

Cot stands still above the bay. The four reach the bottom, get their boards. Start putting on wet suits. Charlie rummages in the food bags.

Ellen's gathering stones.

Ellen Practice, knowledge. More practice, more knowledge.

Rose What?

Ellen Women aren't virgins Rose. Ergo, to have the

knowledge of what a woman is one must practise not to be a virgin. And if the knowledge of what a woman is comes not with the single practice then more practice must be done and knowledge both subjective and objective will be born.

Rose What?

Ellen Dialectical materialism. My mother says . . .

Rose What're you doing?

Ellen What's it look like?

Rose What do you want stones for?

Ellen Target practice.

Rose You're not going to throw them.

Ellen No point being unobserved.

Rose You could say hello.

Ellen I'm shy.

Rose You'll kill someone.

Ellen They're teeny, weeny, weeny stones, Rose.

Rose It's a question of velocity Ellen. Don't.

On the viewing platform.
David picks up a maths instrument box.

David Yours?

   Cot reaches out for it. David holds it away.

Compasses?

   Cot shrugs.

Cot Blue.

David Yeah.

Cot Never seen such . . .

David What?

Cot Blue.

David Exams're over Cot. Too late for revision. Future's set.

Cot Your future.

David What's that mean?

Cot Give them.

David What d'you want compasses for?

Cot Give.

Davey chucks them.

David Suit yourself.

David watches them down on the beach, shading his eyes against the light.

On the beach.

John Jesus can't wait.

Charlie Where's the Kettle Chips?

Rob Girls.

Charlie I'm fucking ravenous.

John See this board. Thinner see. Faster. Got a memory this board. State of the fucking art. I can't wait.

Charlie Need food. Need. Need. Need.

Rob Think they've noticed us?

Charlie Can't fucking live without Kettle Chips. (*Ravening through the bags.*)

John Sun on the rock, Rob. Feel that.

Rob A year older.

Charlie Give us a hand here Rob, I'm dying.

John Old as time, this place, can't get any older.

Charlie Kettle Chiiiiiips. (*He finds them.*)

Rob Us though. Last year we were young.

Charlie Thank you, God. Thank you. Thank you. Thank you. When I'm old and done I'll write my PhD and it will be on potato crisps. Walkers versus Golden Wonder. Sainsbury's Gourmet versus Kettle Chips. In Spain you know. In Spain there's a brand called Papas Lolitas. Just outside Valencia you find them and they are fucking sublime. Deep fried in virgin olive oil so there's not even cholesterol to worry about. Shape. Thickness. Grain of salt clinging. Holy man, I'm telling you. I remember my first Kettle Chip. Major event. Huge. Tufnell Park. Delicatessen. Fucking starving man. Stood by the cash desk. Ripped open the bag. Aroma. Oil. Potato. I mean real potato. It's a clear day outside. Frosty. Blue sky. I take the Kettle Chips out into the cold. Standing leaning against the window in Tufnell Park. I put the Kettle Chip in my mouth. It was beyond crisps man. We're talking orgasmic, I swear to you.

John What the fuck were you doing in Tufnell Park? (*He's munching.*)

Charlie I could be a crisp-taster by profession and I would be happy all my life.

John Army doesn't have crisp-tasters.

Rob Ow!

Ellen Bullseye.

Rose Shit.

Rob You do that?

Charlie What?

Rob fishes a stone out from down his back.

Rob Fucking stone, Chaz.

Charlie I'm eating for God sake.

Rob You d-didn't throw it?

Charlie I'm busy, Rob.

Rob You throw this stone at me?

Charlie I didn't throw the fucking stone, Rob. Why me. Why not him?

Rob He wouldn't throw a stone.

Charlie Neither would I.

Rob You m-might.

Charlie You are getting in my face, Rob.

Rob Think those girls did it?

John What for?

Rob Think they like me?

John Could've killed you.

Charlie The sun. The air. The sea. Best packet of Kettle Chips I've had in my entire fucking life.

Rob Going to all that trouble. Must like me.

John Girls. Leap on you. Lick your teeth. Stick their tongue down your throat and call it love.

Rob I do not see that as a p-problem.

John I'm sitting at the kitchen table. I'm going over what I'm bringing down here. My mother's sitting there with her friend drinking wine. 'Board, towel, wax, leash, fins, fin socks, O'Neill,' I say. 'Condoms,' my mother says. I fucking hate that. 'Three condoms,' she says. 'Don't insult him,' her friend says. 'Two days he's away for.' And she leans across to me. 'Take ten,' she says. And they laugh. I'm dying inside and they're laughing for Christ sake. 'Condoms,' I say. 'Never go anywhere without them. It's second nature,' I say. And my mother goes bright red. She can pitch my mother, but she can't catch. 'You haven't got any,' she says. 'In my bedroom.' 'You have not,' she says. 'Let me know if you ever need to borrow one. KY jelly if you need it.' Stop them laughing. 'Your father,' she says. 'Your father doesn't even know what KY jelly is.' Women. Sex is all they think about. Feel like a piece of meat. Once. Yeah. Just once. I'd like to make the first move.

Rob Nobody's ever licked my teeth.

Charlie Play saxophone, don't you?

Rob I have very l-lonely teeth.

John yells up to the viewing platform.

John Davey?

David What?

John Get down here.

David Won't be long.

John Come out with me, Davey.

David Catch you up.

Rob Must like me to throw stones.

Charlie Dreamer Rob.

Rob When I leave this beach I'll be a changed m-m-m-man.

Charlie A poke's like a shit.

Rob T-t-talking about girls, Chaz. Not talking about b-b-bowel movements. Not talking about b-b-bodily functions.

Charlie Talking about doing it.

Rob Talking ideals. T-t-talking s-spiritual. Nothing spiritual about a shit.

Charlie Depends how long it is since you had one.

Rob She likes me, that's all.

Charlie You, you ballocks, be a miracle if you ever say hello.

   The packet pings.

Fuck. Bloody stone in here. If I hadn't seen that, I could've put my hand in there, picked out a mouthful rammed it in, in expectation of bliss crunched down. Could've broken my bloody tooth if I hadn't seen that. They do that?

Rob W-w-watching us.

Charlie Give them something to watch. Anybody touches these Kettle Chips, they die. Talc?

John Catch.

   Charlie strips off, shivering.

Charlie

   On the baby's bum
   On the baby's knee
   Where can the baby's dimple be.

   On his cheek
   Or on his chin.

Rubs talc over his legs. Arms.

John Davey?

Rob Leave him, John.

John Davey?

Rob leaps on Charlie, rubs the talc all over him.

Rob Should p-p-put it in the suit, n-n-not on you.

Charlie What's the odds?

John Aesthetically?

Charlie There's nothing wrong with my body.

Rob Nothing a transplant wouldn't c-c-c-fix.

Charlie You are a jealous pile of gobshites. (*He heaves up. Grabs his wet suit.*) They watching?

Rob L-looking at me.

Charlie Honed to perfection.

John Hairy, though.

Charlie What's wrong with a bit of body hair?

Rob Bloody apeman, Chaz. P-Pity the woman making love to you.

Charlie What?

Rob Choke on it. Want m-my advice?

Charlie No I don't actually.

Rob Immac. All over.

Charlie Don't want your advice.

Rob Chaz is l-losing it. Chaz is losing it.

Charlie Least I'm not a slug.

Rob Who are you c-c-calling a slug?

Charlie Great white slug.

He lurches for Rob. Rob dodges.

Rob You c-calling me a slug? (*Rob squashes the Kettle Chips.*)

Charlie For fuck's sake, Rob. Look at them. (*He upends the packet. Bits crumble out into his hand.*) Look at that. (*He laps them up.*)

Rob Fucking g-gross, Chaz.

Charlie Pleasure see. Got to take it seriously.

John Wind off the land. Four-foot walls. Glassy. I've been dreaming of this. Wax?

Rob chucks John bubble-gum wax.

Rob You are well sad, Chaz. D-do you know that?

John sniffs the bubble-gum wax.

John Smell of summer. (*John yells.*) Davey?

Rob Breaks my heart this p-p-place.

John's waxing his board.

The beauty.

Charlie There's a sewage pipe doing its business round the corner.

Rob B-b-b-breaks my heart, gobshite.

Charlie Effluent from the farms soaking down off the land. Outflow round the corner.

Rob Sob c-c-catches my throat in this place.

Charlie Not the only thing you'll catch. That sea is a streptococcal soup.

Rob You are such a fucking c-crusty. Man's lost in the c-contemplation of b-beauty, you c-could let him b-be.

Charlie beboos his lips.

You c-could let him, that's all. Your m-mind's a fucking sewer Chaz, you know that?

John Zip me up someone. Davey I'm not waiting for you. (*John gets in the water. The others leash up.*)

On the cliff-top. Rose grabs Ellen's throwing arm.

Rose Don't, don't, don't.

Ellen Jesus, Rose.

Rose Don't be cheap.

Ellen We'll be fossils before they make the first move.

Rose There must be a more subtle way to get what you want.

Ellen Fuck subtlety. Life's passing. (*She crawls over the ledge and down on to the beach.*)

Charlie walks out. Rob's leash comes away from his board.

Rob I got to p-push this Tesco's trolley through 'Utopia'.

Charlie Couldn't get a Tesco's trolley in there.

Rob In my dreams, gobshite.

Charlie's backing into the water.

I'm p-pushing this trolley and the videos, they're playing. They're huge on the m-m-monitors. So the waves, Chaz, the waves – g-g-g, shining, murderous. Like to swallow you, the waves, Chaz. You could smell the brine. Like the parting of the Red Sea it was and me wheeling through with my trolley. Only there's gobshites with hands on either side and I'm p-p-pushing them away. For they're impeding me. Right at the end see, between the tunnel of the waves, there's this board. See? Swallow tail, double rails. The man that shaped that board was a fucking God right, I'm telling you. Immortal board it is. See I c-can have this board if I can get to it. Just have to p-p-p-pop it in my Tesco's trolley and it's all mine. Morey mach HS it is. Knife slender. Have to get to it's all. And I do. See? I g-g-get to it. But it's high and I'm reaching up. Fuck Chaz. I'm reaching and I'm reaching.

Charlie Well?

Rob P-p-promise you the world dreams do. Day like this though. W-world does it. C-c-comes up to your dreams man.

He's still fiddling with his leash. Ellen runs down the beach, stands a little way from Rob. A silence, an avoided look, a look. Sound of fighter planes; one comes over. They're low. Then another.

Charlie Yip! Yip! Yip! Yip! Yip! Yip! Yip!

Cot comes down.

Cot Shit.

Ellen and Rob look up. Planes circle each other. Ellen's laughing. Rob's watching her. Planes go. She looks at him and smiles. He almost smiles. Loses courage.

Charlie You see them! You see them! Sublime.

Rob Jesus!

Charlie She speak to you?

Rob She's . . .

Charlie You speak to her?

Rob Sure.

Charlie You didn't.

Rob We shared t-t-time, Chaz.

Charlie You are seriously unwell, you know that?

Lying flat on the boards. Ducking through the breaking waves. Fighting the surf. Being thrown back. Paddling on.

David's building a fire.

Cot What's this then?

David Barnacle. You crazy?

Cot What's it do?

David It's a barnacle, Cot. What's it supposed to do? It's a mollusc. Molluscs don't do. Molluscs be.

Pause.

Push him off.

Cot tries.

Cot Shit man.

David He eats. He sleeps. He has little barnacles and he clings.

Cot He's good at it.

David You must have seen a barnacle.

Cot I haven't.

David There is no one on this earth who has not seen a barnacle.

Cot shrugs.

Sorry.

Cot What?

David Sound like my father.

Cot I like your father.

David I like him happy.

Cot He not happy?

David Threatened suicide in the kitchen last time I saw him.

Cot Your kitchen's pink, isn't it?

David He'd be happier if I was a mollusc. Add garlic, herbs. Kiss of the frying pan. Pop me in a bouillabaise. Then he could eat me. Know where I was then. Threatened to drown himself because he'd had a dinner party. Asked to borrow my fucking wet suit. Could stand death, he said. Couldn't stand the cold. Don't ever be a doctor. Doctors have a very odd view of life. To a doctor the world is sick.

Cot Small price to pay for job security.

Charlie Fucking surf scares the fucking fuck out of me.

Rob This man goes surfing with his leg off.

Charlie No one surfs with their leg off.

Rob American. Shark got his leg. Now he surfs with one leg.

Charlie Don't get sharks here.

Rob Sharks don't mind sewage. Sharks are not that sensitive.

Charlie John, for Christ's sake, shut him up.

Rob Only b-b-baby sharks, Chaz. C-c-cute really.

Charlie Cute?

Rob Course they have to eat. Eat more often than grown-ups. Baby sharks have to grow. Nibble, nibble, nibble, that's the way the baby sharks go. Know what they like best?

Charlie What?

Rob Know what really attracts them.

Charlie What?

Rob T-t-talcum powder. Well-known fact.

Charlie You're a bollocks, you.

Rob M-man got his side ripped out. Still surfing mind. Bowels falling out. Intestines trailing but he's riding them. Sharks smell.

Charlie You fucking smell.

Rob Cot wouldn't feel it if a shark bit him. Cot doesn't feel pain.

Charlie He feels it.

Rob P-pain's a state of mind, Cot says.

Charlie State of fucking body, man.

Rob Question of interpretation, Cot says.

Charlie Bollocks. Those women there. If they weren't there we'd be talking profundities. Sitting out here waiting to catch one, we'd be talking about the state of the universe. Sorting it out. Sex we'd be talking about. They're there though. Listen to us. What are we talking about? Fucking pain, man. That's what we're talking about. What the fuck happens when they get closer. Talk about sex every six seconds.

Rob Who?

Charlie Girls. Well-known fact.

Back on the cliff.

Ellen See. What they're like, see. They're like knights. They are. Knights on white horses. They're romantic. They are. Give them.

Rose Get off.

Ellen Thought you were cooking.

Rose In the pan.

Ellen Thought you were celibate.

Rose They're my binoculars.

Ellen Lah di da.

Rose looks, adjusts the focus. Ellen shades her eyes.

The one in the black's mine.

Rose They all look black against the sun.

Ellen The one that's the angel. Him in the lead.

Rose See him on the rock. See. I love long hair on a fella. Makes them look gentle. I like a gentle fella.

Ellen Not me.

Rose Hair must be down to his shoulders.

Ellen Anyone I go with has to be strong. You have to be strong in this world. I want a looker. And I want him to want to look after me. Not that I can't look after myself. I can look after myself. Just want him to want to . . . you know . . . And I never want to know I've got him. Don't want him to talk to me too much. He can go off with his mates if he wants. Don't want the soul out of him and if he ever gave it to me I'd spit it back in his face. Don't want to 'know' him. Not get to the bottom of him. Want a bit of mystery to keep me guessing on a dark night. I want him moody. I like a moody fella. Could take the cider down to them.

Rose Sex can't be all you want.

Ellen What I want . . . what there is . . . it's hidden behind a cloud. Take an angel to blow the cloud away and let me see. I've found my angel.

John Jesus, Rob. Jeeeeeesus.

Bobbing like seals. Waiting.

Charlie Shit.

Rob What?

Charlie Something touched me.

Rob Fish.

Charlie What kind of fish?

Rob Robert M-M-M-Maxwell fish.

Charlie They buried him in Israel. He's not down in the depths nibbling at my toes.

Rob He's alive and well and l-l-living in Brazil.

Charlie Seaweed. Seaweed. (*Waves it.*) Robert Bloody Maxwell.

Rob See he pays this poor b-bloke that's about his size and his age. He's got this p-planned six months ahead. Knows he's in trouble doesn't he? P-plans a runner. He says to this bloke, 'Here's a million pounds. In six months' time I want you to be me. I want you to fall off my boat and drown. It's a nice boat,' he says. 'You'll like it. You'll be buried in Israel. We'll say Kaddish. Do what you like with the m-m-million.' And the bloke, he has this six months. And he l-lives. How he lives. Then he gets on that yacht. And pffft. His time's up.

Charlie I wouldn't do that.

Rob I would. Only I'd make them let me have nine months and I'd have a b-b-baby.

Charlie Fuck off.

Rob N-n-n-no. I w-w-w-would find this woman and she'd . . . I'd l-l-l-leave all the m-m-m. I'd leave it to my baby. I'd die happy. (*Shades his eyes and looks to the cliff-top.*)

Charlie Be alright at the start. Be alright then. How'd they walk up the steps to the guillotine? How'd they do that?

Rob Need m-money in this life. My baby'd be rich. I'd walk up those steps. I'd fly.

Charlie Got to grab life. Got to hold on to it. All you've got to call your own and you'd give it away.

Rob L-l-live p-passionately. L-let go l-lightly.

Charlie I won't let go. Not ever.

Rose and Ellen are eating beans on the cliff-top.

Ellen My mother was sixteen when she lost her doughnut. Said she waited till she was legal. She was itching to do it, she said. Lost her doughnut on the bathroom floor.

Rose My mother was a late developer.

Ellen Lost it to the only good-looking boy she ever had. Said that finished her with the good-looking ones.

Rose My mother broke her rosary when she was nineteen.

Ellen Cherry I've heard. Cherry's cool. I like cherry.

Doughnut if you are chubby. Rosary, though? Rosary?

Rose She had this set of white beads. Her communion set, see. Used to wear them as a necklace. And she had it off with the bass guitarist in the Web.

Ellen Never heard of them.

Rose He's dead now. Once they got a record in the Belgian top one hundred. They were at this party, see. And she'd decided. 'Right tonight's the night,' she'd decided. And he had these bandy legs and hipsters and she loved fellas with bandy legs my Mum. Makes them look vulnerable she says. She's a sucker for a vulnerable man my mum. That's her downfall. Said she'd never have done it if she'd known he was going to die. Altogether too bloody vulnerable she said.

Ellen If I was going to die I'd do it. I wouldn't want to die a virgin.

Rose Anyway they did it on top of the coats. And caught his plectrum in her rosary and it broke.

Ellen His what?

Rose Went back the next morning to pick up the bits.

Ellen He go back with her?

Rose He climbed Ailsa Craig and fell off. What comes of bandy legs.

Ellen She's a disaster your mum.

Rose 'We're at the mercy of the environment,' she says. 'Each and every one of us. You're a dreamer if you think otherwise, or a fool,' she says. 'You can't plan. You can only placate the fates, duck, keep quiet and hope the winds of Chance don't notice you and blow on by.'

Ellen Jesus, Rose, you've got to leave that woman. You've got to take charge. I'm not waiting for the winds of chance. No way. I'm going to run my life. I'm going down there. The weather's fine and I'm not waiting till I'm nineteen. Are you coming with me?

Rob My hormones are ruining me. Why do you have to m-make the b-biggest decisions about your f-future when your hormones are at screaming p-pitch? Sat their GCSEs and lost my hormones did.

Charlie Don't know that. Not yet you don't.

Rob Evolution, yeah. Girls are ahead. Sometimes that worries me. Sometimes I think OK. And I see my future and I'm on a beach. And I've got this little blond kid and he's my son. And his mother's making her way in the world. And we're happy me and my k-k-kid on this beach. I've a lot to g-give a kid.

Charlie This is the best bit waiting. Know what I feel?

Rob Peace.

Charlie How do you know that?

John Breaks look better out there.

Charlie These are fine.

John Look at them, Chaz. Tubes out there, see.

Rob Kate's M-Maw.

John Looks wild.

Ellen They haven't done it I bet . . .

Rose You can't tell they're virgins by the look of them.

Ellen They're quite strong these binoculars.

Rose What about love?

Ellen I'm full of love me. I love them already. Love's no problem.

Rose No, no, no, no.

Ellen See this place. This is special. You and me out here. This is magic. You ever tasted beans like these?

Rose Don't see what Heinz baked beans have got to do with having a shag on a beach with some bloke you've never seen before.

Ellen Beauty of them. Breaks my heart. Ephemeral see.

Rose Jesus, Ellen.

Ellen Stomachs and tits. That's us.

Rose Not me.

Ellen And the way they're friends. We're bitch friends. They're friends like it's the ends of the earth, Rose. Look at them.

Rose I'm looking.

Ellen I melt inside Rose. I do.

Rose That's the beans.

Turning round into the waves.

John Set coming in.

Rob Charlie.

Charlie Oh, Jesus. I'm just a style junkie, Rob. I'm freaking out.

Ellen Oh God, oh God, oh God. Look at them. My heart's pounding. I'm sweating. I can't stand it. Come on.

Rose What you gonna do?

Ellen God knows I've tried to be subtle. I'm going to introduce myself. (*She's taking off her jewellery, necklace, earrings and rings.*)

Rose You spent all last night putting that on.

Ellen Think they go for tarts, do you? They listen to Nirvana, they do. They don't want tight skirts and Wonderbras.

Rose You're not a tart.

Ellen They don't know that. Give me the nail-varnish remover.

Rose passes it to her.

Look at him, look at him, look at him in the black. I'm dying Rose, dying. Aren't you dying? I'm dying. If he falls, I'll kill myself. If he's hurt, I'm dead.

Pounding of surf. White, white light.

Charlie Fucking speed.

John Staying with it.

Charlie Fucking rush. I love it.

Rob Power man, see.

John Still running.

Charlie Don't take the first.

John Wait, wait. Now.

Pounding surf. Guitar. White light. John drop knees. Surfs. Then:

Wipe out. Shoulder. Down, down. Need to breathe. Pain. Jesus. Die if I breathe. Tooth of rock waiting for me. Slowing. Stopping. I can see Paradise. Rock doesn't slash me. I'm with the angels. Up through the water. Light through the water. I can breathe. Another one coming. Take it. Take it. Jesus, the speed. Miracle, the speed.

Pulse of light. Pounding surf.

Ellen Like seals. All black and shiny. Not human at all. Like dolphins.

Rose You want to fuck a fish?

David Here. (*David hands Cot a rock.*) Man's ability to use tools. Raises him above the molluscs. Lets him pay income tax.

Cot knocks at the barnacle. Cot hammers the barnacle. It comes away.

Cot Smashed the shell, man.

David What'd you expect?

Cot Didn't want to do it damage.

David I don't believe you've never seen a barnacle.

Cot It's bleeding.

David Can't call that ooze blood.

Cot You white boys, you're all the same.

David This is me you're talking to. This is David here. I'm not some white boy. I'm your friend.

Cot I see them coming from the slaughter house, the blood still on them.

David What slaughter house?

Cot You whites. You sit down to your English tea with blood on your hands that you haven't washed. With your bodies unclean. I've seen you.

David What slaughter house? This is one barnacle.

Cot You should have told me.

David You should have thought. (*He picks the barnacle up, tries to attach it to the rock. It falls.*) Jesus Christ, Cot. A barnacle, Cot, a sodding barnacle. Doesn't even know it's alive.

Cot Knows I've killed it.

David Ceased to know. That's what dead is. If I told you to jump off the cliff, would you?

Cot Take you with me.

David Promises. Promises.

On the cliff-top.

Ellen Look out there. Look at that wave.

Roaring of surf. White light.
David looks out to sea.

David John's going for it. John's flying. Up the wall. Up, up. Come on John. Come on. Come on. Off the lip. Air. Flying, flying.

The surf pounds in.

Ellen Jesus, I'd love to do that. No I wouldn't, no I wouldn't. To be him. Jesus I'd love to be him. Look at him. Like a swallow. Like a flying fish. Like Concorde.

Rose For Christ's sake?

Ellen What do you love, Rose? You've got to love something.

Rose I love . . .

Ellen I love Concorde. Makes my insides quiver. I'm jelly Rose. I'm flying with him. Look at him. Just to be him.

David Riding it. See him, Cot? See him? Gleaming, Cot. Shining.

Cot climbs high on the rock.

Ellen Bet they don't like tattoos.

Rose You haven't got any tattoos.

Ellen Just as well, eh?

Rose You really going to do this?

Ellen I have thoughts Rose. I talk. I never carry them through. I talk. I plan and dream and then I talk some more. What if I went through my whole life and I never ever carried out a single thought that I had.

Rose What if you carried out the wrong one?

Ellen Rather that than the life sucked out of me. Us and them in the whole wide world. The very air's vibrating. Feel it.

White light. Pounding surf.

David Rock'll have you for breakfast. Wave'll have you off. Shit Cot. Come back.

Cot I'm alright.

David The tide'll get you. The folds in this. Break your ankle.

Cot Come here.

David I'm alright where I am. The earth beneath my feet. That's how I like it. Come back down Cot.

Cot Let go.

David Break your leg, man.

Cot Let go of me.

David Rock's not there for your benefit. Jesus Christ.

Wave lashing. Blast of light. David's flung down. Cot falls. Slithers.

Ellen Arms round me. Gentle arms. Gentle eyes looking into mine. And not a harsh face. Arms cradling me. Do I look nice? Would you want to cradle me?

Rose Would it stop you going down there if I did?

David I'm wet. I'm wet. I'm soaking.

Cot You'll dry.

David I don't get wet. Look at me. This is not what I came here for.

Cot What you come for Davey?

David Look after you lot. There's blood on you.

Cot I'm alright.

David You're bleeding.

Cot Barnacles got their own back.

David You hurting?

Cot Naaa.

David Take your T-shirt off.

Cot Fancy me, do you?

David I want to see that.

Cot I bet you do.

David Get septicaemia.

Cot A cut is all.

David Take the T-shirt off or I'll take it off for you. (*Challenges Cot.*)

Cot Means that much to you? (*Cot takes off the T-shirt, barnacle cuts on his chest bleeding copiously.*)

David Bloody things are like razors. (*He gets the medical bag.*)

Cot Doesn't hurt.

David Course it bloody hurts. Can't bleed like that and not hurt. Pain is a message to the brain, Cot. Something's wrong, it's saying, 'See to this part of me.' Pain commands, keeps us safe. Deny it, . . .

Cot What?

David Dangerous thing to do. (*He's fingering Cot's shoulders.*) Way I see it. You don't acknowledge pain, you become numb, not just to the things that hurt you but to every single thing living or dying in this world.

Cot Not the way I see it. World's full of pain. Round every corner, pain. Learn to bear it and you survive. Seen my father grow pale. Seen grey come in and tinge dark circles round his eyes. Seen him sit in the corner of the sofa and cross his legs, so. Not move for a day. Eyes flick sometimes. See a world without hope for him or me, or my mother or my sister. I hate him for that. You can bear pain, you don't lose hope.

David Told me he had a job, Cot.

Cot He's got a job in the slaughter house and grateful. You seen gratitude, Davey? You seen it?

David What's this, Cot? (*He touches the tops of Cot's arms.*)

Cot Stop pawing me. You queer or what?

David What is it?

Cot Scratches.

David Jesus.

Cot Cat got me.

David What's this, Cot?

Cot Cat, I said.

David Who's been at you?

Cot Leave it, Davey.

David You telling me this was the cat?

Cot Cat's a maniac, Davey.

Pause.

Leave it Davey. Please.

David This is a mess, Cot.

Cot Give me my T-shirt.

David Oh shit, oh shit.

Cot Give it to me.

Pause.

You've got to be strong's what I believe.

David Jesus.

Cot How you get strong doesn't matter.

Pause.

David What is it that's happening to us? We were happy little bunnies when we were five years old. We were all the same. Whole class girls and boys. Shiny faced and full of possibility. No stupidity. No disadvantage.

Cot Way you see it.

David I did work experience in a nursery. I saw happiness.

Cot In Milton Keynes were you?

David No colour, class, no dysfunctional . . .

Cot My world there are no nurseries. You lot coming in.
You lot, parents weighing up which school suits.
Supporting comprehensive education as long as the
school's in at the top of the lists. As long as it can boast an
Oxbridge entry. You lot. Incomers. You don't live where I
live now. When was the last time you talked to Jake or
Kevin or . . .

David Grunt, they don't talk.

Cot The split population that we live in starts from birth,
Davey.

David They had the same opportunities we had. They had
the same teachers.

Cot For fuck sake, Davey.

David They do this to you?

Cot It's not that simple.

David You want to grit your teeth and bear it. You want
to smile through pain. Here. Practise. I could use Savlon.
I'm using this. Calendula. Burns like buggery. You want to
tell me how you got those cuts?

Cot No.

David Smell. Marigolds. You want pain. I'll give it to you.
(*He slaps the cream on the barnacle cuts.*)

Cot Thanks, Davey

David What did the cat use on your arms, Cot?

The cream goes on Cot's shoulders.

Razor blade?

Cot Toothpick.

David Not funny Cot.

Cot shrugs.

Here. It's dry. (*He gives him a spare sweatshirt.*) Always pack a spare. Never know what might happen.

Cot You'll make someone a good wife.

David Talk to me, Cot. Tell me.

Cot See this. All this.

David I'm looking.

Cot What do you see?

David Sand, sky, rocks, sea. (*He's watching John.*)

Cot Beauty?

David If you like.

Cot smiles.

Cot Paradise?

David shrugs.

Paradise though? While your mother tours the cathedrals of Southern England. And your father cooks rhubarb preserve with sweet Cicely.

David Yes, yes. Alright. Paradise.

Cot sweeps an arm over the whole landscape.

Cot Little streak of blue is all.

Ellen You coming?

Rose A woman is tits and a crack. Tits and a crack is all.

Ellen You're halfway there then.

Rose I can't go down to the beach.

Ellen Sumo wrestlers got tits, Rose. They don't think they're women.

Rose In Burma I'd be a beauty. In my mind I'm a freak, Ellen. When he started, that man with the books I was really grateful. Jesus someone fancied me. Then I noticed. Not once. Not once has he raised his eyes above my wrist bones. I dream of Burma sometimes.

Ellen They've got mortuaries there I bet. You could move. Oh God Rose. Look at them. Swallows on the water. Indulge me. I need you. I'm frightened on my own. We've been together all our lives Rose. I'm not saying shagging's compulsory. Please. Please. Please. Let's just have some fun.

Rob screaming in from the sea.

Rob Jesus. Fucking wave took me across the sand. Ripped me across. Couldn't stop. Dragging me it was. I'm fighting it. Grazed every piece of bare skin on my body. Fucking wave playing with me. Need a new wet suit. Jesus. (*He shades his eyes. Looks to the cliff-top.*) Wish they'd come d-down.

David Shit.

Rob Think they'll come down?

David Hope not.

Rob Tide's up. Waves here're dying. John's gone to c-catch the breaks on Lady Kate's M-Maw.

David He's what?

Rob Don't start.

David You let him?

Rob C-c-c-ouldn't stop him.

David Should have gone with him.

Rob C-c-can't k-k-keep up with him. Your p-p-preserve.

David What's that mean?

Rob C-c-can't keep up with him.

David Kate's Maw's too far.

Charlie Best time ever, ever. Honest to God. I'm starving. That John out there? Way out there? Hole in my gut. Get the food out, Davey. I'm dying.

David I can't see him.

Rob Someone else up on the cliff.

Charlie Bloody Piccadilly Circus.

Rob Past the g-girls

Charlie Man?

Rob What's he d-doing?

Charlie Looks like t'ai chi.

David shouts out to the waves.

David John. John.

Charlie I need to eat.

David We'll wait.

Charlie I'll die.

David John. Get back here.

Charlie Feed me. Feed me.

David shouts.

David John. Get back here now.

Charlie He can't hear you.

David John. John. John.

Shower of stone from the cliff-top.

Ellen Jesus.

Rose Oh shit.

Ellen The cliff's moving, Rose.

Rose There's someone up there.

Ellen Bloody cliff.

Rose Oh God, Ellen, it's him.

Ellen You can't see.

Rose It is. It is. I know it. Met your mother at the fish and chip shop. Talked about the wonders of your poetry over the battered cod. 'Rhythm of the sea through it Mrs ehhhh Hammond. Hardly a seaside town this, Mrs ehhhh.' She told him where your rhythm came from, didn't she? She bloody well told him.

Ellen He likes your work better than mine, he always has.

Rose He likes my wrist bones. He doesn't notice my work.

A moment.

Ellen Come on down.

Rose I can't.

Ellen Stay here then.

Rose I can't.

Ellen Stay here then.

Rose I can't.

Ellen Come on. Come on. Run.

Rose He'll see me.

Ellen (*pulls Rose's hand*) Run. Run. (*Begins to run down the cliff path.*)

David Jo-o-o-o-o-hn.

Alone in the sea, John is sitting on his board.

John Barreling. Jesus. There're barrels out here. Never seen. Go back John. Go back. Force of that. Beat your brains out. Jesus. Breaks my heart. I can do this. I will do this. If I do nothing else in my life. (*Comes round.*) OK. OK. OK. OK. OK. Now. Now. Now.

White light. Pounding surf. Drop knee. Music.

Blackout.

Act Two

Rose Pitching a fucking tent. Maybe it's not him. Bang,
bang, bang. Does it the old-fashioned way. Big daddy-
longlegs. That's him. His big daddy-longlegs bending this
way and that. Big bendy bendy. Trousers creased at the
groin. Old creased trousers. Poor trousers. Oh Jesus, Jesus,
I hate him, I hate him. Poor bastard. It's not him. Can't be
him. Shit, shit. I can smell him from here. 'This is a
coincidence, Rose.' 'Certainly is sir. Come for the fossils
Sir?' 'Second only to Lulworth Rose.' 'Certainly is Sir, for
fossils Sir.' 'So Rose?' 'So Sir? Why didn't you go to Mull?
Why didn't you spend half-term with your wife? Why did
you come here chasing me? You're ruining my life. You've
got a musty smell. You've got a shiny skin. You've got a
kind kind smile. You've got little wrinkles round your
eyes. You've got a crepey neck that matches your crepey
trousers, Sir. You're a long, long way from home. Must be
desperate to come this far.' Shit it isn't him. It can't be him.
Stand still till I get a look at you.

> *Sound of stones falling. Waves. Bird cries. Bright, bright
> sunlight. A plastic shuttlecock sings to and fro,
> repetitive. Charles hits the shuttlecock up and up and
> up.*

David Started out thinking I didn't want to go.

Cot What?

David My father said 'Do this for me.' His hands were
shaking. 'I do this I'll help him.' That's what I thought. Go
along a path; don't have to go in the door do you? So. I sat
this exam. That's all, didn't tell . . . you, him. Didn't tell

them. Big old hall. Spent the whole time counting the fucking bricks didn't I. Didn't fucking think I'd get in did I?

Cot What're you saying to me man?

Beat.

When we go to college we go together Davey. That's the plan.

David My father is celebrating. What am I supposed to do? You fucking tell me.

Cot Shit Davey.

Ellen Where are you? My swallow, my concorde. Can't see you. These won't focus. Bloody things won't focus. Where are you?

David Wiped out last year. Jellyfish got me. Portuguese Man of War. Looked like a dirty blue plastic bag. Don't get Men of War here. Get a lot of plastic bags. Shoulder and ribs it got me. Couldn't draw a breath. Grey fog coming toward me. I slip under that. I slip under. John got me out. Fuck it. (*Roars.*) Joooohn.

Charlie Yes, yes, yes.

Rob Jesus they're so close. So close.

Beyond the remains of the picnic the lines of a badminton court are marked out. Rob's looking in the girls' direction though they're hidden from him behind a rock.

Hello. (*Waves racket at Rob.*)

Rob She s-s-smiled at me. We shared a smile her and me.

Charles serves a delicate chip of a serve. Rob smashes it down. Charles dives to retrieve it . . . misses. Crashes into David.

David Fuck off, Chaz.

Charlie Sorry, Davey. Flies'll get this. (*He rummages in the remains of the picnic.*)

Rob Chaz!

Charlie lobs the shuttlecock to Rob.

Charlie Food'll rot in the sun. (*Bends down to pick up the food.*)

David You got worms?

Charlie Best eat. Be on the safe side.

The shuttlecock is driven at Charles. He drops his racket. Drops the sandwiches, shields his face.

Shit. Rob! (*Drives the shuttlecock back into play. The game continues.*)

Surf. Bird cries. Sound of stones falling.

Ellen Shouldn't do it. Shouldn't go near them. Whole nation gets its sex education from the front of the newspapers courtesy of the Conservative Party. They'll expect us to supply oranges and plastic bags. Stick to poetry, Ellen. Poetry's the coming thing. Jesus where is he?

Cot's at the water's edge.
David's on his hands and knees with a plastic bag picking up jellyfish.

David It's a fucking plague. Saps belief in a benign God. Shit. Can't fucking see him.

Cot He missed lunch, Davey, is all.

David Pain in my gut. He's dead, Cot.

Cot Surfing the point is all.

David What's up with your arms?

Cot Leave it, Davey.

David You some kind of case, Cot?

Cot You watching for the man or what?

David What the fuck are you playing badminton for?

Charlie What're we playing badminton for, Rob? Davey wants to know.

Rob Playing badminton for f-fun, Charlie.

Charlie Fun, Davey. Rob says.

  David flings the jellyfish.

Shit.

David Bull's eye.

Rob Shit, Davey.

Charlie What'd you do that for?

David You see him?

Charlie What you fucking well do that for?

David Do you see him?

Charlie No.

David You're not even looking, gobshite.

Charlie Fucking maniac.

Rob Where'd they go? Where's the jellyfish?

Cot Standing on them.

Rob Shii-iiit.

Charlie Could have gone in my eyes maniac.

Rob Ow, ow, ow, ow, ow, ow.

Charlie Could've fucking blinded me. (*Charlie pushes David. Back and back.*)

David Come on. Come on.

Cot Leave it.

  A moment.

David Get the fucking coastguard. John's dying, we need the coastguard.

Charlie If there was anything wrong we'd know.

David How would we know, for Christ sake? He carry a flare in his wet suit, does he?

Charlie Get off my back Davey.

David All you see is a sports arena.

Cot Leave it Davey.

David That's Nature out there. She's brutal. Lying in wait there. If he dies, Charlie. I'll kill you. If he dies . . .

Rob Jesus, Davey.

Charlie I can't keep up with him.

David You don't try.

Charlie I don't have the board.

David You don't have the courage.

Charlie You been in the water?

David Nothing wrong with your board.

Charlie Davey . . . (*His hand's on David's shoulder.*)

David Take your hands off me. (*Beat.*) Take your fucking hand off my shoulder.

Rob's dancing in the sea.

Rob My feet. My feet. Killing me my feet. B-b-b-b-burning up. My feet are on fire. Shit, shit, shit. D-d-don't ask any of you if I'm alright. All I ask out of life. B-b-be on a beach. Burning up. (*Slides a small jellyfish out from his shorts.*) Ow, ow, ow, ow.

Ellen If he comes back I'll be different. I'll be good. I'll be silent in the face of adversity. I'll believe there's a God and never eat fish again. If he comes back I'll give my velvet DM's to Jane Dale and go barefoot through the halls of the Milton House Hotel and let the manager throw me out and not say a word. If he comes back. Jesus. I won't speak to him if he comes back. I won't utter a word. Not unless he speaks to me. I won't. I will be meek and mild. I will stay in and talk to my Nan on a Sunday. And clean her mess off the bathroom floor and not say a word. And I hate that. I really, really hate that. If he comes back.

Charlie What's that?

Cot What?

Charlie Look.

Rose There.

Ellen You see him?

Rose There look.

Ellen Oh God.

Rob There there look.

Charlie That him?

Rose On his board.

Cot Lying flat.

Rose There. Look.

David You see him?

Rob You blind?

Rose He's tired.

Ellen Jesus.

Charlie Come on, come on, come on.

David touches Charlie on the shoulder in apology. Charlie shrugs him off. Rob runs. Charlie follows. David watches.

David Stopped paddling, hasn't he? You looking at me.

Cot Naaa.

Ellen I'm a limp rag. My legs won't hold me. Oh God, Rose.

Rose undoes the top of one of the bottles of cider.

Rose You're all talk. (*She passes the cider to Ellen.*)

Ellen I know. (*Ellen toasts Rose.*)

Charlie and Rob have John by either arm hauling him out of the water. Charlie's got his body board.

John I'm f-f-f-freezing. (*Shivering uncontrollably.*)

Cot Jesus, look at you. (*Cot unleashes John.*)

David Towels!

Charlie Sit down.

John Should've been there.

David Both been frozen then.

John Can't move. Feet are stuck.

David Get the fucking towels. (*He goes to unzip John. His hands are shaking.*)

John Get on with it.

David Get the towels 'fore he dies of hypothermia.

> *Shivering increases as Chaz wrestles John out of his wet suit. Big performance from Chaz.*

Charlie Yes. Yes. Yes. It's coming. It's coming. (*He unpeals one leg of the wet suit. Pulls. Falls flat on his back. Arms outspread.*)

Yes. Yes. Yes. The earth moved. Can he go for a second. Yes he's going for a second. (*Works on the second leg of the wet suit.*)

John Leave my fucking leg on.

> *Charlie fetches towels and dry clothes. Rob lights a fire.*

Should've seen me Davey.

David We would like to have seen you.

John Went out to the Maw.

David Need a four point three if you're going to stay out that long.

John You angry?

David I'm controlling myself.

John Eight feet out there. Ten. There were barrels out there. Going through. Should've been there. The light Davey.

Rob B-b-b-birth canal.

David Cut the metaphysics.

Rob Read an article.

John My first barrel. I'll never forget that. Never. Out past the Maw.

David Could have got yourself killed.

John You find out what matters out there.

David What matters John?

Silence.

Tell me.

John shrugs.

Charlie You forgot?

John Have to be out there.

Rob Message from the deep. Courtesy of God. Will you accept the charge? No fuck off. Line's engaged.

John I'm coming back in. Can't feel my feet, I thought, won't feel the rocks. Rocks waiting for me. Could've amputated my feet and I wouldn't have known. Count my toes.

Charlie Ten toes.

John You'd tell me if one was missing.

Charlie I'd tell you.

John Fight I had to get back in. Rip's alive against me. 'No you don't,' it's saying. 'No you sodding don't.' Gets so I don't lift my arms. Strength gone from them. Rip takes hold of me. Jesus I could've slept. Piss in the O'Neill, keeps me warm.

Charlie I touched that.

John Beautiful weariness I feel.

Charlie He let me touch that.

John Thought dies first. You know.

David No.

John Telling you. Just life left. Small need to live. Nothing outside that. None of the crap. Obscene need to live. And an awful . . . joy.

Charlie D'you have an erection?

Rob Jesus, Charlie.

Charlie Well-known fact erection . . . binky bonk.

John Waves coming. Sets of five. Mess. Swell. No wind. Catch the third. Can't come round for the first two. Too cold. Third one's no more than slop. I shout. You don't hear. This girl's round the corner. All I can see is this girl. She fills my mind.

Rob What g-g-g-girl?

John All I want in the whole world and she's there on the beach waiting for me. I wave. She doesn't see.

Rob W-w-waiting for me, John.

John A mirage is she? And I'm out there and I think if I live I will I'll spend the rest of my life looking for her.

David She's a dog this, girl.

Rob W-w-warning you, John.

David You couldn't see from out there.

John I saw.

David Ballocks, John.

John I thought you'd come for me. 'He'll know I'm in trouble,' I thought. 'He'll get in the water. He'll come and help me.' You didn't, did you?

David As you see.

John's gripping him hard.

John I'd have done it for you.

David I know.

John You see the fog from the beach?

David Birth and death all in one afternoon. Lucky little bunny. What a busy day.

A moment. John gets up and walks away from David. Davey picks something up. Sings to himself.

'T' was here my summer paused
What ripeness after then
To other scene or other soul
My sentence has begun'

Cot What you got, Davey?

David Fossil. Blue clay see. Like stone but it isn't. Soft. See. Beauty this. Warm. Here.

Cot Feels good.

David Best I've ever found. Intricate see. Want it?

Cot Sure, but . . .

David Keep it.

Cot Funny how warm it is.

David Cut yourself, don't you?

Cot Betrayed him. Didn't you?

David All be the same in a million years' time. Not even a pattern on a rock. Should trust us, Cot. We could help.

Rose is watching the cliff.

Ellen Wish I could hear them. (*Ellen tickles her under the arms.*)

Rose Don't do that.

Ellen Don't you wish you could hear them?

Rose Who's that?

　Ellen shades her eyes. Looks where Rose is pointing.

Ellen Don't know.

Rose Ellen, Ellen, Ellen, Elen.

　Ellen slaps her.

What the fuck did you do that for?

Ellen My mother always does that to me before an exam.

Rose What for?

Ellen I get hysterical.

Rose I'm not hysterical.

Ellen Not now you're not. Give.

Rose Don't ever hit me again.

Ellen Don't ever make me. (*Ellen tries the binoculars.*) Sun's in my eyes.

Rose It's a man, isn't it?

Ellen It's a black shadow is all.

Rose It's a man.

Ellen Maybe it's a man. It may not be 'the' man.

Rose Who else would it be?

Ellen You want me to make a list?

Rose He's looming over my youth, Ellen.

Ellen Tragedy queen you are.

Rose What'll I do if he comes down.

Ellen Smile and say hello.

Rose Piss off.

Ellen You will Rose. Smiley, smiley, smiley. It's what comes of having a mother who works in a mortuary. (*She pulls Rose's lips into a smile.*) Rigor mortis. Have you ever ever in your life said what you felt?

Rose I hate you.

Ellen applauds.

Ellen Now, go up there and tell him to fuck off. (*She pushes Rose.*) You have to take it on, life. You only get one go.

Rose So you think it's him?

Ellen I'm all washed. I smell fresh. I've got the cider. I've got plans for the evening even if you haven't.

Rose I'm not up for this.

Ellen It's not you that has to be. That's a joke. Laugh. Please.

Rose has the binoculars to her eyes.

Shit Rose. Shit. Stop it. Please. Oh shit. (*Ellen sinks down on the rock.*) I'm all deflated. Look at me. Haven't even got to the climax yet and I'm all anti-climactical. Looming over your youth's fine. Why does he have to loom over mine?

Guitar.
The boys are round the fire. The wine's passing. David's
cooking. Ellen and Rose are some distance away. The
shadows are long on the beach. The sun's behind the cliff.

Charlie Love 'em and leave 'em, I say.

John You are not an expert, Chaz. You got your sex
education from . . .

Rob Chris Eubank.

John The Elephant Man.

Charlie Where do you get yours from?

John Brittany. There was this woman. She was thirty-five.

Rob J-Jesus, a geriatric.

John She was French. The French don't get old.

David Beware the farting of the fabulist.

John Actually, this is true.

David Is it actually?

Charlie My mother's thirty-five.

Cot I'm going to die at twenty-seven. Joplin, Morrison,
Hendrix, Kurt Cobain, me.

Charlie Wouldn't shoot myself.

Cot 'Better to burn out than fade away.'

> *John starts to sing the Nirvana song, 'Come As You*
> *Are'. The others join in. John leaps up on to a flat rock.*
> *Mimes a microphone. Rob mimes and mouths a guitar.*
> *David air-drums. Charlie on keyboards. They sing it*
> *through. Cot raises a wine bottle in a toast.*

Cot Kurt Cobain.

Charlie leaps down from the rock. The others follow.
John stage-dives. They catch him. Grab bottles.

All Kurt Cobain.

David Absent friends.

Cot Don't want to see thirty. Right now I can see that there's a way to live and it's the right way and we none of us are doing it. None of us see. But we might. Long as we can see. Never want that to change. Don't want to go on living and be dead inside. Always have to see that there's another way. Always have to try and reach that.

John I've always fancied his mother.

Charlie She's trouble, my mother.

Rob John had sex with a wrinkly.

Charlie My mother's boyfriend's too young to be my father.

Rob Did you, John? B-B-B-rittany. Did you d-d-d-do it?

John The rains came down.

Rob I'm not asking for a weather report.

John Skies opened.

Rob I want a weather report I phone the S-S-Surf Line.

Charlie Shut the fuck up, Rob.

John Whole campsites flooded. Tent's awash. Two o'clock in the morning.

Rob And?

John We took to the road, Dad and me. Left the tent and the bikes. Took off to find a logis. Right?

Rob Go on.

John We've been walking a bit. Jesus I've never been that wet. Feet sloshing around in my Caterpillars. Trench foot imminent. My dad's got his head down. You know, grim. Plodding on. All of a sudden this car pulls up by us and this woman . . .

David What kind of a car?

Rob Doesn't matter what kind of a c-c-c-car, for God's sake.

David You don't know.

John Don't I?

David He doesn't know.

John It was a bloody Citroën.

David No, it wasn't.

John It was France, wasn't it? French drive Citroëns. It's the law in France. That's how they've got a car industry and we've got the Japanese.

David It wasn't a Citroën.

John How do you know? Were you there?

Charlie Coitus interruptus or what?

David Wasn't a Citroën.

Charlie You some kind of Puritan or what?

David Define Puritan.

Charlie What're you chatting about?

David Using big words again, Charlie.

Charlie You starting?

Rob He's talking about w-women, let him talk.

David He knows ballocks about women.

Charlie Knows more than a sheep-shagging faggot.

Rob For fuck sake, John, g-get on with the story.

John Don't know if I want to.

Rob My tongue's hanging out, m-m-man.

David It was a Buick, sky blue and white.

Rob So this woman pulls up in a B-B-Buick.

John A Citroën. Shit.

Rob What the hell does it matter what the c-c-c-c-vehicle was. Did you fuck her?

John Yes.

Rob Where?

David Where? Where? Where? For Christ sake where do you think? Do you need a diagram?

Charlie She was French, wasn't she?

David The difference is geographical. Not anatomical. Jesus.

Charlie Could've been the bathroom couldn't it? Or the hall. Or the dining-room table if she was French. French aren't limited to bedrooms. I want details.

John She took me back to this house.

Charlie I hope this is going to be disgusting.

Rob And your father?

John My father was knackered.

Charlie Shagged out.

Cot Girls are still there.

David This is not their place.

Rob It's a p-p-public beach.

David Next thing we know the bloody National Trust'll take it over, ruin it totally.

Rob Keep your voice down.

David I'm not the one telling dirty stories.

Cot They're not looking.

Charlie Why not?

Rob Shut up, you might learn something.

David Be a first if he did.

Charlie What is it with you?

David What're you looking at?

John Mirage maybe.

Rob H-h-hands off, J-J-John.

Charlie Go on, John.

John We go through this hall and there's this replica of the Last Supper, life-size, all laid out in this enormous space. Apostle mannequins in all their robes. Hands reaching out to bread baskets. This is weird, I'm thinking. My father doesn't even notice. Stumbles on to the sofa. Big black sofa. Right where Jesus should have been sitting there was a skeleton. My father wishes him goodnight. Thought he'd walked in on a dinner party. The woman takes me upstairs.

Rob And?

John And.

Pause.

David I saw that film at the Curzon.

Rob You did not.

David It was a Buick.

A moment.
John's laughing.

Rob You lied to me.

John I gave them the story.

David Time it takes to get a film together you must have lost your virginity before your ballocks dropped.

Rob snatches a brand from the fire.

Rob You fucking lied to me.

John No one makes anything up. It's all just life edited down.

Rob You lied to me, ya ballocks.

John It happened. It happened. (*He runs across the beach.*)

Rob You fucking lied, you bastard. (*He chases him.*)

John In life, see, in life she drove a Citroën.

Rob I suppose they paid you royalties.

John Film-makers. Load of plagiarists, aren't they? Never pay their dues.

Rob You'll pay.

David French cinema's got taste. Wouldn't touch you with a bargepole.

John runs to the rock above the girls to get away from Rob. Rob rushes to the rock.

Rob Wanker.

*John jumps down the other side right on to Ellen.
Knocks her flying. One of the bottles of cider breaks.
Ellen cuts her hand on the glass. She doesn't notice.
She's totally winded by the fall.*

Rose Oh God Ellen, look at your hand.
Ellen?

Rob I've k-k-killed her.

The others come pelting over. John lifts Ellen to her feet.

John It's you.

Ellen Who?

John I saw you.

Ellen Did you?

John I was out there. I watched you.

Ellen Did you?

John I waved.

Ellen Did you?

John You were standing there. So I waved.

Ellen How lovely.

*A moment.
David looks at John with Ellen in his arms. Rob comes
in close.*

Rob D-d-d-d-don't J-J-J-J-

David Let her breathe.

John You alright?

Ellen Sorry.

Charlie Whole bottle of cider wasted.

Ellen I'm really, really sorry.

David Gobshite jumped on you, why are you sorry?

Rose You're bleeding.

Ellen looks at her dripping hand.

Rob Apologise.

John What's up with you.

Rob Apologise, I'm telling you.

John I'm really sorry. Get off, Rob.

Charlie That's how you get tetanus, isn't it? Worst place to cut yourself. You get tetanus from a cut on the palm of your hand. Specially near the thumb. Knew this bloke once got a cut near his thumb. Died in screaming agony. That was tetanus.

John Died in front of you, didn't he Chaz?

Charlie Practically in my arms.

John His sister knew this fella knew a bloke that had a friend that was a gardener.

Charlie Gardeners die of tetanus. It's a well-known fact.

David I've antiseptic by the fire. (*He heads off.*)

Charlie Need a tourniquet.

Ellen My shorts. Rose?

Rose S'fine.

John leads Ellen away.

Rob Hey. Hey.

Ellen What? What is it?

Rob stands there. Doesn't speak.

Sorry?

Beat.
Rob struggles to say something.

Charlie Sorry. Sorry. Rob?

Rob goes on staring.

Ellen Is he alright?

Charlie Come on, Rob.

John You alright? (*He puts his hand on Rob's shoulder.*)

Rob Don't t-t-t-t . . . (*Knocks John's hand off. Grabs his wrist.*)

Beat.

John Rob?

Rob lets him go. Walks away down to the edge of the sea.

Ellen What's wrong with him?

Charlie I'll . . . Sorry. (*He follows Rob.*)

Cot's staring at Rose.

Rose What're you looking at?

Cot goes on staring.

Cot You.

Rose Why? Please . . . (*Stretches her sleeves down as far as they'll go.*) Oh God. (*Crosses her arms over her chest. Hands in armpits.*) Don't.

Charlie Rob?

Beat.

Come on Rob. Wait up.

Ellen What did I do?

John Need to get that seen to. (*He takes hold of her arm. She winces.*) Sorry. You hungry? Got plenty food if you'd like some.

Ellen calls back.

Ellen Rose.

Rose What?

Ellen We could bring cider, couldn't we?

Rose picks up the remaining cider bottle.

Rose Shit.

Cot's digging a hole in the sand.

Cot Pardon?

Rose Sorry.

Cot Go on.

Rose I'll wait.

Cot Don't want anyone else cut.

Rose looks up to the top of the cliff. Rob's looking back at John and Ellen.

Rob Want to s-s-s-smash him, Chaz. He's my friend and I love him and I want to give him pain. All the things that c-c-c-came into my head to say to her. C-c-c-couldn't say them. Wanted to be close to her is all. B-b-b-breathe in the s-s-s-smell of her. She is everything I ever d-d-dreamed of. What she thinks of m-m-me. Thinks I'm a c-c-clumsy ballocks that's what she thinks of me. Thinks I'm a f-f-f-fool. And she's right. A fool is what I am.

Charlie Look at that.

Rob Tide's right out.

Charlie Think it'll ever turn?

Rob Not yet.

Charlie Desolate.

Rob Breaks your heart.

By the fire.
John's tending to Ellen's hand. David's opening another
bottle of wine.

Ellen You've got wine.

John His mother slipped him a bottle. 'Don't tell your father.' His father slipped him a bottle. 'Don't tell your mother.' He nicked a couple of bottles and didn't tell either of them.

Ellen They bring you here?

John Been coming here for years. Used to be one car would bring us all. We grew. The folks get the cars out. Haul us down here. Dump us. Come back next day.

Ellen Fond parents.

John Not bad. How's that?

Ellen Comfy. Doesn't hurt.

John David's the medical man, usually.

David Don't get blood in the ratatouille.

John Wine?

Ellen Please.

John No cups.

Ellen Fine. John, is it?

John S'right.

Ellen Smells good.

David My dad makes it.

John Ragout of vegetables. That right, Davey? Sun-dried tomato paste. Aubergines unsalted. His father leaves the bitter juices in. David had a set-to with a Portuguese man o' war last year. Freak plague of them round this coast. Man o' war won. That's a dead man sitting there cooking supper.

   Pause.

Ellen I'm really sorry.

John Not half as sorry as we are. A toast. The dear departed.

David I will drink to elderflowers.

Ellen Why?

David Their season is short. (*It's Ellen he toasts.*)

Rose with Cot.

Rose See the way the firelight goes. See. (*She's pointing up at a small glow on the cliff-top.*) He's got the coffee pot in his hand.

Cot Can't see that.

   The glow dims.

Rose S'put the coffee pot on the fire. He's had four cups of coffee. He'll be up all night. Think he's looking down here?

Cot Friend of yours?

Rose Don't know. I can't even really tell if it's a man or a woman. We've been here a lot her and me and there's never been another soul. Turning into Brighton Pier. I mean, d'you come here often or what?

Cot *They* do. *My* first time.

Rose It's quite ugly really. My mum brought us first time February. 'Cause of the fossils. She's into remains, my mother. Drove all night. Cliff's raw in February. Slag heap. I'm thinking we drove all that way for this. Then you look. It kind of enters into your dreams. I long for these rocks. See the way the waves break. I'd rather be here than anywhere else on earth. You know. (*She shivers.*)

Cot Cold?

Rose Bit.

Cot Want to go to the fire?

She looks at him.

Rose Not yet.

He takes his sweatshirt off. Puts it round her shoulders.

You don't have to do that.

Cot Don't feel the cold.

Rose Thank you very much.

Ellen Cheers.

Ellen toasts John. Their eyes hold. David grabs a potato out of the fire. Throws it to John.

David Catch.

Reflex action, John catches the potato. Burns his hand.

John Shit. (*Drops the potato.*)

David Butterfingers.

John What'd you do that for?

David Thought you might be hungry.

John You burnt my hand.

David I've got some nice ointment for burns. You just come over to my side of the fire and I'll see to you.

Rose with Cot. They nearly kiss. She breaks it.

Rose I don't . . .

Cot Sorry.

Rose No, no I just . . .

Cot I didn't mean . . .

Rose No of course not. I . . .

Cot What?

Rose Think he can see?

Cot From the cliff-top?

Rose Not with his naked eye, of course.

Cot Watching the sea and the dark. Path of the moon.

Rose Look. Look.

The small fire burns bright. Then it's doused.

Cot 'Nother cup of coffee.

Rose I don't want him looking at me. Whoever he is. Don't want him spoiling the night.

Cot Come on.

He holds out his hand. She takes it. They walk together into the shadows.

By the fire.

David You want to be careful with him. He's like a little dog, John. Leaves his scent on every lamppost. Know what I mean? He's led a sordid life. Not a fit companion for a girl of your obvious . . . talents.

Ellen You're a bit of a shit, aren't you?

David's got the bottle.

David Scared of the dark. Susceptible to nightmares. 'I'm cold, Davey, cold. It's dark Davey, see.' Want me to put my arm round you? And in those days he had a lisp. 'Yes Davey, please.' 'Come on Davey play.'

Ellen I don't understand.

David

'To lose him – sweeter than to gain
All other hearts I knew
Tis true the drought is destitute
But then I had the dew.'

Ellen Emily Dickinson.

John I'm not the one moving on.

David Aren't you?

Down the beach.

Rob I don't ever want to feel this empty again.

Charlie A slight stammer can be very attractive. Women like diffidence in a man.

Rob They should have had a beautiful child my folks. My sister's beautiful. Then they had me. A love like theirs. How can that produce me?

Charlie Hardly fucking Frankenstein, Rob.

Rob They met in the Louvre. My mother says my father shone. Been together since that day. I don't shine.

Charlie You're alright, for fuck sake.

Rob John's always going to and you will.

Charlie What?

Rob Land on your feet.

Charlie Come back to the fire.

Rob I don't mind. Lot of the time I don't.

Charlie Smell the food, Rob.

Rob I had a girlfriend once. Six years old. The two of us. Could hardly get a word out then. She was blonde. She listened. Never finished a sentence for me. Didn't matter how long it took me, she waited. I loved her. Caught her back of the church. Six years old. Waste ground. Lined up all these boys from our road. Kissed them one by one. Lifted her skirt. I tried to stop her. She laughed at me. G-got them all laughing at me. 'Petersfield. Petersfield.' Local loony bin. Shouting at me. I told her mother. She never spoke to me again.

Charlie The mother?

Rob No. Where you going?

Charlie Need food, Rob.

Rob Could you fancy me?

Charlie Oh, Jesus.

Rob Come on. Honest.

Charlie Got any Kettle Chips?

Rob No.

Charlie I couldn't fancy you. Nothing personal. Shit. Come on.

Kneeling facing each other, Cot and Rose in the moonlight. Rose running her hands over the tops of Cot's arms. Very softly.

Rose Oh Jesus, oh Jesus, oh Jesus.

Factually.

Cot Came up to the school with friends. Not this lot. Beautiful place. Red brick and the oldest something or other tree in England. Listed building the Music faculty's in. Listed school. Top comprehensive. I love the place. Folk travel miles to get to it. It's the ones that come from the estate. That's who you expect the trouble from. I got it from my friends. Came a big split. Don't know why. Happens. Split turns sour. I look at them. They hate me. Took the compasses to me. Paul started it. Frank, Cato, Aaron. Sons of my parents' friends. Every morning. I sit down. They start. No one sees. They're invisible. I'm invisible. Form teacher's talking about school uniforms, litter, parents' signatures in day books. Fretting about shoes. Through the jumper. Through the shirt. Compasses filed to a cutting edge. Pain. Alright. Alright. Day after day after day. I learn to expect it. I tell no one. Not them. (*He nods towards the fire.*) Start a gang war that way. I care about them. Someone get killed that way. Deal with it myself. Key to it is pain. They think to master me. (*He shrugs.*) First it was hard. Piece of cold metal. Cutting into your own flesh with it. Spewed the first time I did it. Practised though. I make my cuts deeper than they ever go. Still they don't go away. 'Wanker, wanker, wanker.' Whispering. Then they cut me. Small movement is all. Used to make me cry. I cried in front of them. Head down. Snivelling in the classroom. Still invisible. Well.

See. Now. I don't cry any more. Now I don't flinch.

Rose They've stopped Cot, haven't they?

Cot I sit in front of the mirror. I have a towel by me. Black towel. Case there's blood. Sit cross-legged in front of the mirror. Night-time this is. I've got compasses in a box with a velvet lining. W. H. Smith. They're good ones. Sharpened them like they did. Lay the box at my side and the towel. You have to breathe right. You don't get the breathing right and you can't do it. Since I was a little kid. Sore stomach, headache, earache my mother made me breathe through pain. Breathe pain away. Can't sleep even. 'Just breathe,' she'd say. 'Sleep will come.' Pick up the compasses. Concentrate. Breathe. Make the movements slow. Take as long as you like. Don't look at the real hand. Look in the mirror is all. Keep looking in the mirror. (*He makes the gesture of the cut. It has grace.*) Doesn't hurt see. Triumph. It's done. Then the pain comes. Greet it. Feel the course of the pain through my whole body. Follow it. Let the mind take it. Lead it down. Ground it. See my face in the mirror. There is no pain in my face. Yukio Mishima. Know him?

She shakes her head. He shrugs.

That's who I am sitting there. Pain is my philosophy. In answer to the fear. In answer to the wasted belief of my father's generation. In answer to the grey and the worry. Pain is my colour and my constant and my hope. Then they stopped. Got nothing out of me. I won. They play football in the mornings and come in late to registration. They've forgotten about me.

Rose Here. (*She touches his shoulder.*) These are fresh cuts.

Pause.

Cot Wouldn't like it if one day I couldn't stand it any more. Would mean I was afraid. Mean I was grey like them.

Rose I'm really, really sorry.

Cot No need. Way of life is all. (*He shrugs.*)

By the fire.
Ellen has the bottle. John strokes her hair.

Ellen Make me shiver.

John Your hair sparks under my hand.

Ellen Oh God.

John Real sparks of fire.

Ellen I'll have to change my hair dye.

John Like a cat.

Ellen D'you like cats?

John Little cat I've got. Sparks fly from her fur. Quiet little thing. Stays there all night. Just stroke her. Quite, quite quiet.

Ellen I'm not quiet.

John Sorry.

Ellen I wish I was. I wish I was biddable. I wish I was really, really small. But I'm not. I'm sorry. I'm noisy. I'm drunk now. But I'm just as noisy when I'm sober. It's horrible.

Rose takes a long swig from the cider bottle. Then turns it upside down.

Rose Oh dear. We used to play Peter Pan and Wendy her and me. I was always Peter.

Cot That's nice for you.

Rose No, no, no. I wanted to be Wendy. Do I look like a boy?

Cot laughs.

Why is that funny?

Cot You don't look like a boy.

Rose In your opinion.

Cot Boys are . . . different. Honestly.

Rose Look at these. (*Holds out her wrists.*)

Cot What am I looking at?

Rose They're my wrist bones.

Cot So they are.

Rose I think they're drunk.

Ellen You alright?

Rob Very w-well, thank you.

Ellen You don't look it.

Rob I'm fine. Fine honestly.

Ellen shrugs.

Rose heads for the stairs.

Cot Where are you going?

Rose Up.

Cot Careful.

Rose Have I drunk more than you?

Cot Much more.

Rose I don't feel sick yet.

Cot That's good.

Rose I have to take my life into my own hands. Is that the drink talking?

Cot Might be.

Rose Is it making sense?

Cot I don't know.

Rose I have to see a man. I have to go up the stairs.

Cot It's a long way up.

Rose Very, very, very long way. I have to get there very, very fast or I might not get there at all. (*She starts to run up the stairs.*)

Ellen's lying on the ground flat out. Hand spread over the sand. Wine bottle held safe.

Ellen Hear that?

John No.

Ellen Have to get down. Right, right, right, right down.

He does.

David Anybody eating this?

Charlie Me.

Ellen Throbbing. Feel it? 'Live, live,' it's saying.

John Feel it out there. All you can feel.

Ellen Take me out there.

Charlie I can't hear it.

Rob S-s-striving. See. There's a B-B-Britain that you live in that's physical. And this. Hear it? No matter what. All the shit. See. It's still there. Striving for Ut-t-t-topia.

Charlie Puke, Rob. Garbage. Utopia? Maudlin load of fucking bilge Rob. 'Ut-t-t-topia?' 'Utopia' is a surf shop off the Portobello Road.

Rob It's s-something at least.

Charlie What you hear? The rocks and the sands and the strata fighting, warring yeah. Utopia? Stillness. Sameness. Stagnant Utopia is. What you hear. The Lords of Misrule screaming out their war cry.

David slow-handclaps.

You? You know nothing.

Rob Want the world to stay still t-till I reach it.

Ellen Oh God I want to go out there. I want that more than anything in the whole wide world.

Charlie Davey wouldn't go in the sea. Not even to find Heaven guaranteed.

David Put some food in your mouth, why don't you?

Charlie You'd have let him die and not lifted a finger.

John I wasn't dying.

Charlie He thought you were.

David You didn't go in after him.

Charlie You're the one that could.

David I could not.

Charlie Don't ever want to be like you. You can hear it. Live. Live. It's all you can hear.

David Are you calling me a coward?

Charlie Did I not say it loud enough?

David You're stupid Chaz. You know that? Fucking breadhead.

Charlie What're you chatting about?

David You want power Charlie, that what you want?

Charlie What the fuck are you saying to me?

David Police, is it? That where you're headed?

Charlie Fuck off.

David Army?

Charlie Fuck you.

David Army, though?

Charlie What?

David Army, Charlie?

Charlie Yes, yes, yes. Army. Yes. What's wrong with that? You tell me. What's out there? You tell me.

David Violence, Charlie?

Charlie Way you see it.

David What else is it with a gun in your hand. You tell me. You fucking tell me.

Charlie You have to . . .

David What?

Charlie Someone has to.

David Not one of us. Come on, Charlie.

Charlie There's nothing out there. A beach he's heading for.

Rob Beach is what I'd like. Library's where I'm headed.

Charlie I don't fucking want that. You're alright.

David What's that mean?

Charlie Daddy's alma mater opening out her arms to you.

David You heard?

Charlie Don't believe everything I hear.

John Thought you were asleep.

Charlie 'S it true Davey?

Rob What?

Charlie Oi, is it true?

Rob What the fuck?

David Scholarship, Chaz.

Charlie All the same to me.

Rob What scholarship?

David I got a fucking scholarship.

Rob Jesus, Davey.

Charlie Of course you did.

David You want violence?

Charlie No.

David You want it.

Charlie Fuck off.

David Come on, hit me.

Charlie Fuck off, Davey.

David I worked, fuck it. You smoked dope in the park.

Rob All d-did that.

John Could do with some now.

David You reap what you sow.

Charlie Jesus, Davey.

David You want to hit. No reason. Just hit. Hit. Hit.
Come on, hit me.

Charlie Put down that ladle and I will.

David Come on. That's what you want. Come on. Hit me.
Hit me. Hit me.

> *Charlie does.*
> *Beat.*
> *Ellen touches David's arm. He shakes her hand off.*
> *Almost turns on her.*

Charlie Had enough?

David Come on. Come on.

> *Charlie knocks David over.*

Charlie Know why I hit you?

David I asked you to.

Charlie Talking about hope. You ran out man. What that
said to me. You accepting that scholarship, said I was a
scumbag no-hoper. Said I never would have any hope. We
were in there together yeah, you broke it.

David Better than medicine, Rob. Should have seen the
old man's face. Between a rock and a hard place, Rob.

Rob What?

David Did I have a choice?

> *Rob turns away.*
> *John lifts David's head up from the sand.*

David There. See.

John What?

David I told them. How d'you think it went?

John You alright?

David Sand in my eye.

John Don't rub it. Pull the lid down. (*He captures David's hand. Tends to the eyes.*)

David *Brief Encounter.* I'm Celia Johnson. You're Trevor Howard. Rachmaninoff. Old war horse of a concerto. Brings tears to my eyes.

John Better?

David Think this is the end?

The others go back to the fire. Charlie helps himself to food. The others watch him.

Charlie What? I'm hungry. What?

Rose I'm going to be sick.

Cot Not now.

Rose You're not even panting.

Cot Long way to go.

He runs up the stairs. She follows.

Rose I'm going to get fit after this. I'm going to be so different. I'm going to wear short sleeves for life.

Cot Gets cold in winter.

Rose I'm never ever going to smile again.

Cot I like your smile.

David gets to his feet. John touches David's cheek.
A moment.

John Can't expect them not to be hurt.

David You go out there, that's your responsibility. You go out further than . . . it's your responsibility not mine.

John Come back to the fire.

David Nothing happened today, did it? Nobody died. Nobody's fucked anybody yet. A day on the beach in early summer is all. Beginning of the fucking end darling.

John shrugs.

John What?

David Them. Amazing grace and the mountain goat.

John They get scholarships did they?

Beat.

David

'To winter to remove
With winter to abide
Go manacle your icicle
Against your Tropic Bride'

John You're in danger of becoming affected.

David 'Embrace danger.' Isn't that what Chaz says. I will if you will.

Beat.

I'll go back and hold my father's hand, because it needs holding.

John Can't live his life for him.

David Couple of shazas tolling the death bell. I would

have liked us to have ended with some ceremony at least.
All of us. She flaunts in, Ellen. Shazas on the beach,
jellyfish in the sea. Choice, choice, choice.

John Up to you.

David What?

John How it ends.

On the height.

Rose This is it see. These are the possibilities. It could be
him and I could confront him and tell him what I think
and he'd be chastened and he'd go and never 'look' at me
again. And then we could make love you and me. And
I'd be a woman and I'd be able to think. Are you
shocked? Don't say anything. Or. I could knock on the
door of his tent and he'd come out and it wouldn't be
him and that would be a relief to see some perfect
stranger standing there. And I'd think what a fool I am
and you'd think what a fool I am and then we'd not
make love because you wouldn't fancy a fool and I
wouldn't fancy a man who thought I was a fool and I'd
probably throw your cut-up arms in your face because
women can be cruel. Don't say a word. Or. It could be
him and he'd see me and I wouldn't have to say anything
just be silent and dignified and off he'd go and I'd be
silent and dignified with you and we'd not make love
because silent and dignified people don't have to and that
would be alright. Don't say anything. Or. Or it could not
be him and we'd make love because you saw I was
disappointed and you wanted to make it up to me. Now
you can say something.

Silence.

Say anything.

Cot Seems to me that while it all hangs in the balance I'd be a fool to commit myself either way.

Rose See I think we'd make love and you'd never ever have to cut yourself again.

Cot That simple?

Rose Like an American film.

Cot Too simple.

Rose Never know.

Cot My father works in a slaughter house.

Rose Does he?

Cot Just testing.

Rose My mother works in a mortuary. We were made for each other.

Cot You crying?

She shrugs.

Rose . . .

Rose I can't . . . He's asleep. Whoever he is. Dreaming? What do you think?

Cot wipes the tears from her face.

Think I'm his dream? Know what I think?

Cot You drank too much.

Rose I think he needs his dreams. Whoever he is.

Cot Come back to the fire.

Rose You should laugh more, d'you know that? (*She runs down the steps.*)

Come on.

David throws Ellen a neoprene vest.

David I'll take you in.

Charlie That's my vest.

David Better than nothing.

Charlie You going in?

David What if?

Charlie In the dark?

Rob Yeeeeees.

John Let's go.

Rob Let's do it.

Charlie There's things in there.

David There's things out here.

Charlie It's dark for Christ sake.

David See the moon on the water.

Rob Clear as day.

David Don't stray from the moonlight.

Charlie I'm hungry. Maybe I'll just . . .

David You're coming.

Cot's holding Rose.

Rose I live awful far away.

Cot I like the way you talk.

Rose Awful far, though.

Cot We could meet here sometimes.

Rose Maybe you could visit.

Cot Want to sleep by the fire.

Rose Will you visit?

Cot Will you sleep by the fire?

Rose I will if you will.

By the fire on the beach the others are all zipped into wet suits. Charlie's building the fire up.

Charlie Need a blaze to guide us back.

Ellen Be cold in the night.

John Sleep by the fire. (*He runs his hand down the length of her hair.*) OK?

Ellen OK.

John Ready?

David Ready.

John Ellen? (*Takes her hand.*) Davey –

David Tide's turning.

Rob Surf's up.

John In off the rocks.

Charlie Jesus!

By the fire.

Rose What?

Cot Take care of this.

Rose Compasses? (*She opens the box.*) They're very ordinary.

Cot What did you expect?

Rose You'll just buy some more.

Cot Maybe I will.

Rose Give me all your money.

  He empties his pockets.

Now you can't can you?

Cot Nice night.

Rose Nice and clear. Pretend. (*She kisses his shoulder.*) All gone, see?

Music.
A path of moonlight on water.

Rob Sometimes d-d-don't you think? Don't you just think?

Charlie What?

Rob You c-could conquer everything.

Ellen See if silver could live, this would be it. When I come out I'll have silver all over me.

  John laughs.

David I'll roast bananas when we get out . . . cinnamon, chocolate, cream. What God can do with a cow?

By the fire.

Rose Touch me.

  Cot looks at her. Slowly raises his hand.
  The light fades to blackout.